The Coffee Boys'
Step-by-Step Guide to

Setting Up and Managing Your Own Coffee Bar

Visit our How To Website at www.howto.co.uk

At www.howto.co.uk you can engage in conversation with our authors – all of whom have 'been there and done that' in their specialist fields. You can get access to special offers and additional content but most importantly you will be able to engage with, and become a part of, a wide and growing community of people just like yourself.

At www.howto.co.uk you'll be able to talk and share tips with people who have similar interests and are facing similar challenges in their lives. People who, just like you, have the desire to change their lives for the better – be it through moving to a new country, starting a new business, growing their own vegetables, or writing a novel.

At www.howto.co.uk you'll find the support and encouragement you need to help make your aspirations a reality.

You can go direct to www.setting-up-and-managing-your-own-coffee-bar.co.uk which is part of the main How To site.

How To Books strives to present authentic, inspiring, practical information in their books. Now, when you buy a title from **How To Books**, you get even more than just words on a page.

To access the free videos that accompany this book make sure you visit www.coffeeboysguide.com

The Coffee Boys'
Step-by-Step Guide to

Setting Up and Managing Your Own Coffee Bar

How to open a coffee bar that actually lasts <u>and</u> makes money...

John Richardson & Hugh Gilmartin

howtobooks

Published by How To Books Ltd
Spring Hill House, Spring Hill Road,
Begbroke, Oxford, OX5 1RX, United Kingdom
Tel: (01865) 375794. Fax: (01865) 379162
info@howtobooks.co.uk
www.howtobooks.co.uk

How To Books greatly reduce the carbon footprint of their books by sourcing their typesetting and printing in the UK.

First edition 2010
Reprinted 2011

British Library Cataloguing in Publication Data
A catalogue record for this book is available from the British Library

ISBN: 978 1 84528 327 8

Produced for How To Books by Deer Park Productions, Tavistock
Typeset by TW Typesetting, Plymouth, Devon
Printed and bound by Bell & Bain Ltd, Glasgow

NOTE: The material contained in this book is set out in good faith for general guidance and no liability can be accepted for loss or expense incurred as a result of relying in particular circumstances on statements made in this book. Laws and regulations may be complex and liable to change, and readers should check the current position with the relevant authorities before making personal arrangements.

Mixed Sources
Product group from well-managed
forests and other controlled sources
www.fsc.org Cert no. TT-COC-002769
© 1996 Forest Stewardship Council

Contents

About the authors

JOHN RICHARDSON

John Richardson started his career with coffee shops at the age of 14. His first job was within a legendary ice cream and coffee shop in the coastal town of Portstewart. Along with his brother, he worked (less than diligently it has to be said) for the princely sum of 60p per hour. At this level he was possibly overpaid. But he didn't agree. As he and his brother sat slumped over the counter on the wet and windy days when it was quiet they would idly calculate how much money the business was making. Like nearly all employees past, present and future, they arrived at a figure of about £500 of net profit for every £1,000 that was put in the till. Slightly indignant at these huge profits that were being made they would pop another stolen ice cream Flake into their mouths and dream at some stage in the future of one day having a business like that themselves . . .

Never forgetting this dream, John went to university and undertook a business and marketing degree and by the age of 26 he owned the largest sandwich business in Ireland. A sad case of over expansion and ignoring many of the fundamentals of business meant that by the age of 28 this business was broken up and sold off.

Somewhat chastened he then moved into a variety of other businesses including chip shops, garden centres, coffee shops and restaurants. The lessons learned from the sandwich business stood him in good stead and many of these businesses became highly successful and garnered many awards. An interesting and somewhat greed-driven venture into the internet in 2001 wasn't so clever though and helped illustrate to him how important it is to keep focusing on the fundamentals of what you really know about.

In the summer of 2005, John sold his stake in all his trading businesses and established a consultancy business aimed primarily at the coffee shop industry. His clients range from single-site espresso bars to multi-site chains with a few restaurants thrown into the mix for variety. With Hugh Gilmartin (and a few other associated Coffee Boys), he helps produce anything from full turn key coffee bar operations, to assistance with training, marketing and operational systems.

He, along with Hugh, has previously written a book for existing coffee shop owners titled *Wake Up and Smell the Profit – 52 Guaranteed Ways to Make More Money in Your Coffee Business* (HowtoBooks). John speaks, with Hugh, about the business of running coffee shops throughout the world.

John lives in Bangor County Down with his wife and daughter. He is also the author of *Dream On – One Hacker's Challenge to Break Par in a Year* (Blackstaff Press Ltd), a book about a golfing challenge that he undertook and which most of the golfing world regarded as impossible.

HUGH GILMARTIN

Hugh Gilmartin has been in the coffee business for 25 years. He advises key people in the hospitality and retail sectors on how to maximise the profitability of their coffee businesses – something that is becoming increasingly more important. He runs Northern Ireland's largest coffee distribution business with his brother and is always keen to adopt new ways to persuade his customers to buy their coffee from him, modelling the best business practices and developing ideas from different countries and cultures.

He was the first Irishman to present his ideas at The Speciality Coffee Association of America's annual conference many years ago when America was significantly ahead of the rest of the world in terms of the coffee revolution. He has written dozens of coffee marketing related articles as resident coffee guru with several national magazines and with his friend and 'Coffee Boy' collaborator John Richardson they help and educate their clients on how to make, and crucially maintain, profits in what he terms 'The Business of Coffee'.

Hugh is involved in several businesses specialising in marketing and branding and how to develop the sensuality and experience of overall coffee related operations. He has been a Board member of the Speciality Coffee Association of Europe since 2006 and is well known in UK coffee circles.

Hugh lives in Belfast with his wife and three daughters and at home his opinion is rarely asked about anything – even coffee!

He hasn't written any books about golf but still believes he can beat Johnny in a head to head match.

Introduction

Before we start – a little bit about why we wrote this book and the reasons why we wrote it in a certain style.

This book is, we feel, a little different from many of those that currently exist within the marketplace. There are a large variety of books out there that all promise to help you open your first coffee shop/coffee bar/sandwich bar/ restaurant/lunch bar and most of them provide sterling advice. In fact most of them provide such decent advice that we actually genuinely recommend you buy them. There are lots of specifics within this industry and lots of viewpoints that you need to see before you can fully immerse yourself in your new business. As our somewhat dubious heart surgeon analogy (see page xiv) shows, there really is a huge amount that you need to learn.

Our perspective to opening a coffee shop (or any business like this – we'll deal with definitions later) is based on a very different view point to most other books though. The usual formula for these books arises when someone who has owned one or two coffee shops decides that they want to write a book about their experiences to try and help others. This is an admirable ideal and the resulting book is generally very good at explaining all the myriad dealings with planners, accountants, landlords and environmental health officers that form the rich tapestry of opening your first shop.

What we do is take all of our accumulated knowledge from hundreds of different clients and our own businesses and try to really emphasise the key concepts that WE think are important. Planning advice, legal advice and even, to a limited extent, financial advice should all come from professionals within those areas. We want to help you get into the industry with your eyes wide open as to the actual realities that you will face and, more importantly, an understanding of what you really need to focus on.

Our experience comes from a huge variety of sources. We've learned some very hard lessons running our own businesses in the food industry and have had some incredible successes as well as epic failures. We've worked with and alongside

Michelin starred chefs, world championship winning baristas as well as vastly successful business men and women with dozens of sites covering pubs, restaurants, coffee shops, restaurants and even fast food.

We regularly set up turn-key coffee bars for a variety of clients, so we deal with, on a day-to-day basis, the exact problems that you will be dealing with if you venture into this industry. It's this experience that prompted us to produce this book and it's this experience that makes the book a little different from some of the others that are out there which may actually give you more practical advice. As we say above please read them too, but please, please pay close attention to the key concepts in this book, and if you come across a piece that you feel repeats a previous section then be aware that there is a reason for that – it's because it matters.

The book is divided into four parts.

Part One shows you the good and the bad of the industry. It's about illustrating what a great industry it is to work in as well as making sure you grasp just how tough it can be. This point is crucial. Week in and week out we get emails from owners who are within the first few months of their business and already feel that they have aged ten years. It can be brutal but it can also be great, so read this section carefully to put a little context around the dream of your first shop. What this section will also do is, hopefully, let you step back and view things from a slightly different perspective in terms of what you actually want from the business. Too many people rush into a new business without clearly articulating what the rules of operation will be for themselves, and exactly what they want out of it in the long term.

Part Two is to do with key entrepreneurial traits. Within the consultancy side of our business we rarely find businesses failing for any of the classic reasons like location or the economy. Most of the time they fail because the owners simply aren't managing their enterprise like a business. These six characteristics are what we ultimately end up working on with many of our clients. To fix food, coffee, service, recruitment, marketing or any other specific you must usually first fix the thinking of the owner first. Unless you can apply these skills you will not succeed – it's as simple as that. And the most important one is pig headed determination.

Part Three explains **the great formula**. This formula has evolved over the last 20 years as we have operated our own businesses and observed others who have succeeded, as well as those who have failed. Success leaves clues, and what the formula does is extrapolate those clues and arrange them into a usable seven-step process that you can apply to your business. In essence the formula is as simple as this:

Passion – all great businesses start with a passion to produce something great (rarely is that great thing a pile of money).

Taste – great passion creates the drive and vision to produce great tasting food and drinks.

Positioning – this is where reality steps in. Where will you position this great product within the market and will there be a market for what you create?

People – none of this works without an understanding of people at a very deep level. We are a people intensive business directly serving the end customer with an emotive product.

Marketing – no matter how good your product is, it won't sell unless you can let people know about it and entice them to buy into a little of your magic.

Systems – if you can't wrap decent systems around your business you have no business. You've simply created a job for yourself.

Money – ultimately (but only after everything else is sorted) you must focus on the money. Too often this is ignored within the industry.

Ignore even one part of the formula at your peril as we'll explain to you with a few scenarios.

Part Four takes you through the step-by-step process that you'll need to go through to actually get open. It's not easy to open a coffee shop so you'll need to make sure you have your pig headed determination face firmly strapped on.

But the book doesn't stop there. When we wrote our first book we discovered an alarming statistic – less than 10% of people ever read past the first chapter in a business book. To try and circumvent this we produced our first book, *Wake Up and Smell the Profit*, in a lively 52 chapters format with lots of true stories to help illustrate our points. This, we are delighted to say, seems to have been very useful for our customers and means that the book has never been seen as a daunting business book with lots of dry theory.

This book is different though. We had a much clearer objective with this one and we have a lot of key points that we wanted to get across. It couldn't be another

52 tips and techniques because that would make it too easy for people to perhaps skip a few of the crucial sections. So alongside our endless true stories this time we decided to produce an online video which helps to illustrate these key points in a different style. To access these videos all you need to do is visit: www.coffeeboysguide.com and enter your email address. You'll then have full access to these videos as well as a minefield of extra information to help you with setting up your business or with the management of your existing business.

There is one last thing to remember as you read this book. We tend to use the term 'coffee shop' to describe all the various permutations of what we do in this industry. The problem is that there are a variety of different sub-niches within this. So if you're thinking of setting up a coffee bar/espresso bar/coffee house/café or even a restaurant, please be aware that most of what we say is totally inclusive of all those concepts. You may be amazed to know just how many of these rules and the formula apply equally to fine dining restaurants or fast food joints. So what you mustn't do is think 'Oh that doesn't apply to me – my model is or will be different'. It almost certainly won't be.

Café Culture

THE HEART SURGEON STORY – A SOMEWHAT DUBIOUS WAY TO ILLUSTRATE A POINT

Using a tremendously in-depth piece of research (we typed it into google), it's quite easy to find out how long it takes to become a heart surgeon – 12 to 14 years. So that's 12 to 14 years to learn how to do one little thing incredibly well. Even as we write this we can clearly hear all the heart surgeons around the world throwing their arms up in despair at the ludicrous comparison we're making, but assuming that you aren't actually one of those surgeons yourself, bear with us for a minute or two.

So what is the job of a heart surgeon? Well thinking back to biology at school the heart seems to be a wobbly lump of muscle that has a few tubes coming out of it. Arteries bring blood away from the heart and veins bring it in (or was it the other way round – who knows and indeed for this slightly ludicrous comparison who really cares?).

When something goes wrong you would have to assume that the surgeon basically deals with these tubes and various valves and other red flappy bits that may (or indeed may not) be present. He fixes the things that needs to be fixed, occasionally has his brow mopped by an attractive young nurse, pauses every so often to close his eyes and appreciate a particularly moving piece within the opera that he is listening too and tries really, really hard not to shake his hands and cut a bit that he shouldn't cut.

But it's really all contained within a very small space and ultimately his skill is focused on making sure that he knows everything about that organ to a very high level.

It's the same with nearly all professionals. They spend years and years (long after their primary degree) learning how to get really good at their niche and then they charge a quite enormous amount of money for their time to help you out in their area of expertise. But here's the big wake up call – particularly as far as accountants are concerned. Even after all these years of relentless practice and study, they very often do not actually know exactly what sorts of margins and percentages you should be aiming for within your little coffee shop. Time and time again we come across clients who have been advised by their accountants to have business targets that are 100% wrong for this type of business.

But the real kicker is that when most people (I'm sure YOU don't fall into this category) decide to set up their little coffee shop, their actual understanding of how the business works is extremely limited. Our heart surgeon takes 12 to 14 years to learn that one skill really well, our accountant takes about ten years (and still makes mistakes), and the average coffee shop owner remortgages the house on nothing more than a dream, a bit of 'you go for it' from a few friends, and the hope that he or she can learn on the job.

Here are just some of the key skills that you actually must learn.

- Accountancy – never just rely on your accountant's advice

- Marketing – and no it isn't just advertising

- Recruitment – you need to recruit great people

- Training – the staff need to perform well for you

- Psychology – you'll have to deal with a LOT of people

- Operational management – the whole thing needs to run smoothly

Arguably many of those skills, on an individual basis, require just as long to perfect as does becoming a heart surgeon. So bear this in mind if you're thinking about opening a coffee bar and think 'how hard can it be?'

Part One

The Good and the Bad of the Coffee Shop Industry

GOOD COP

Owning a coffee shop genuinely is one of the most rewarding 'jobs' in the world. Many parts of the dream that drives people to open their first coffee shop actually are true. You can, if you manage it correctly, create a business that is rewarding both financially and from a satisfaction basis. You can create somewhere that people actually want to work in and that can become the hub of your local community.

If you have a love of food or coffee (and ideally both) it can allow you to indulge this whilst making a living at the same time. And if you're clever you can create a model that 100% supports a great lifestyle that allows you to indulge these passions without having to spend hours slogging away producing the actual goods yourself. In short it can, if you're careful and follow the right rules (conveniently we explain them in this book), create something that is truly indulgent.

The catering and hospitality business is, in general, somewhere that always seems a better place to work on the outside than it actually is when you're involved in it. Some jobs within it are truly terrible and require long hours for very little rewards and, in certain circumstances, a certain exposure to danger. Hotel managers work about the longest (and most anti-social hours) of any profession on the planet (excepting junior doctors for a few years). Dealing with drunks in bars is pretty unpleasant, as is serving them fast food in a small window of opportunity before they stagger home or are arrested. Restaurants require a high initial capital cost and you're at the mercy of temperamental chefs and customers who stop visiting during recessions. They also require expensive and regular re-fits to keep them looking fresh.

So if we imagine a long line with all the jobs within the industry lined up in terms of pleasantness, it would be reasonable to assume that running a bar, or a kebab shop, in a bad neighbourhood might be at one extreme end and at the other end is the coffee shop in a nice area. And trust us – we know. Between us we've either owned or managed bars, restaurants, burger joints, fish and chip shops, sandwich bars, a variety of retail operations, and lastly a variety of coffee shops.

It will come as no surprise to you that we have stuck with coffee bars. They are, in our ever humble opinion, the most pleasant part of the hospitality business. We're assuming that since you're reading this book you're pretty much already sold on this fact, but should you be swaying between opening a kebab shop and a nice little coffee shop, let's list out a few facts for you about coffee shops.

■ The opening hours and comfortable environment is the most pleasant within the entire hospitality industry. Whilst there is increasingly a market for staying open after six o'clock in the evening, this is entirely optional and never involves properly late nights. A restaurant or night club may seem glamorous when you're in your 20s, but as friends and colleagues of ours will testify staying up late and dealing with party goers is somewhat tedious when you hit 40.

■ You rarely, if ever, have to deal with drunks. Again this is shifting slightly and, as a result of licensing changes, a few clients are introducing wine onto their menus, but in general the people who may have a drink are unlikely to have a 'skin-full' and start tearing up your seats or telling you that 'you're my bessssst friend . . .'.

■ The main emphasis on the business (but not all) is Monday to Friday. This doesn't apply to all sites but there is no other business, with exception of a sandwich bar, within the hospitality industry that can fit so closely to the classic working week.

■ You will find that, of all sectors within the industry, a coffee shop is the easiest in which to attract decent staff. This is a huge one. The difference between expecting people to make coffee and have a nice chat with customers and persuading them to stand behind a counter a fry fish is like the difference between Mother Teresa and Genghis Khan.

■ The margins in coffee are great. Starbucks have done us all a favour – regardless of what some industry pundits may say. They have conditioned the public to be prepared to pay decent money for a cup of coffee which allows sites in expensive locations to make economic sense (but only up to a point). Many areas of the catering industry suffer from a poor pricing to margin ratio in terms of what the customer expects to pay for the core product. Fish and chip shops are a classic example. The cost of fish is huge and yet the public still thinks of it as poverty food. Pizza is the opposite. The actual cost of production is small and yet the public is prepared to pay a lot for it. Coffee shops sit much closer to the pizza end of the spectrum than the fish and chip end.

■ A good coffee shop can become a cornerstone of a community. With the pub industry declining and a huge reduction in the number of local post offices, a coffee shop is the logical meeting place to replace these two bastions of the community. Not only does this make financial sense for you, it can also provide a nice warm feeling of satisfaction.

So the rewards genuinely are huge, but only if you play it properly. It took us a long time to create coffee shops that worked properly around our own lifestyles. It would be fair to say that it is only a relatively small selection of operators who achieve their goals or make their dream a reality. One outstanding case is someone we'll call Dick.

The true story of Dick

Dick operates a coffee shop in a busy and highly seasonal coastal town. Dick has enough trade during the winter to break-even, but the real money is made in the summer. His fellow business owners historically all expect to be quiet during the winter and pray for good weather in the summer so that their tills will ring loudly and long enough to help them through the next winter. Sometimes they have a great year and sometimes they don't, but they all remain united in the understanding that summer is when you work. If the customers are good enough to be there in the summer then the accepted reasoning is that the owner needs to make the effort to be there. That's just the way it works. Mess with it at your peril.

But Dick isn't really all that keen on this idea. He has a wife and a couple of young kids, a nice house with a big garden and most importantly of all he has a boat. And to be honest he'd actually rather be on the boat in the summer rather than standing in his shop selling ice cream and coffee to hungry tourists.

So Dick has changed the way that he operates his business relative to his competitors and fellow traders. Dick works relatively hard during the winter to tweak his shop and make sure it is fresh and has some new and exciting products in place for the summer. He works on his systems and makes sure that all his finances and financial controls are in place. He works closely with his young manager to ensure that she really understands the key important factors within the business. But he still manages to spend lots of time with his family.

When the summer comes though his plan really kicks into action. Every morning he arrives in to work, just like all the other traders. But by 11.30 am he has left the business, content that everything is under control, and is happily sailing his boat or spending time with his kids while they are off school.

Dick has created a great business that works for him – not just for his customers but for him. That is the holy grail of the coffee shop industry.

BAD COP

A little field trip suggestion

Before you open your shiny new business, particularly if you are burdened with idealistic notions of 'not being in it for the money' or perhaps that other gem 'I just want to make enough to live – I don't want to be greedy', take a little trip down to your local courts when the bankruptcy courts are in session. These truly are the most terrifyingly depressing places known to man. What you find here amongst the pomp and ceremony of the legal profession are truly broken men and women. People whose dreams have been shattered in the most brutal way. People who have thrashed around for months without sleep desperately trying to fend off the inevitable, borrowing, grasping, selling and often gambling their last few pounds to try to find a way out. Some of these people have broken marriages, are about to (or already have) lose their houses.

They sit outside with their solicitor patiently waiting their turn. The solicitors shift between consoling language and engaging in pleasant conversation with colleagues from other practices who they haven't seen for a while. They mutter, as respectfully as possible, about holidays to France and whether they did get round to buying that new Jaguar or not. The client sits there quietly in despair. Some are seeking yet another adjournment, but that's all dependent on the mood of the Master on that day. Will they be granted another few weeks to make a few more last ditch attempts, or will the Master have a hangover or simply have reached the end of his tether with the relentless line of incompetents that he sees sitting in front of him?

Take a really good look at those doomed clients. Have a look at their clothes, observe the lines in their faces, see if you can catch the faint stench of last night's whisky that provided two hours of fitful sleep before they woke up again.

We know you won't do this, but you really should. Because the first time you decide that 'marketing is tacky', or you think that you don't really need to focus on the numbers any more because you seem to be putting plenty of money in the tills, we want you to stop and think back to those wretched souls and about how you really don't want to be one of them. You do NOT ever want to be one of those guys.

The reality of a great coffee shop truly is great – no doubt about it but the flip side is unfortunately somewhat harsh. Dick and plenty of people like him do manage to create a wonderful business (of varying sizes) to work for them, but for every Dick there are generally about five Doras (see page 8) who don't have it right.

The heart surgeon analogy we use may offend heart surgeons but in essence there is huge truth in it. This is a tough business and there are no guarantees that it will work for you. The American small business guru Michael Gerber has calculated that only 20% of small businesses survive the first five years. Of those 20% that survive a further 80% will fail in the next ten years. That's 96% of start-ups failing within ten years – a staggering and humbling statistic.

Our experience would very much bear this out. Between us we have worked in the industry for nearly 50 years and we have seen a tremendous amount of businesses come and go in that time. What makes you think you're so special that you can succeed?

The entire emphasis of this book is to make sure you do succeed and that you do form part of that 4% who have a great business that works for you over the long term. But it starts with accepting the harsh realities that it is tough out there and that you will have to be very focused. We'll keep reiterating it throughout the book, but the formula is borne out of hard won experience. It came about because it works. Not just for us, not just for a couple of clients but for hundreds of businesses that we've been involved with, worked with or advised.

The true story of Dora – a cautionary tale

'Dora runs a lovely little coffee shop in a busy little market town. Dora's business makes a small amount of money and is, superficially at least, the fulfillment of a life long dream. Dora always wanted to own a coffee shop and remained frustrated for a long time in her previous career. When the opportunity finally arose to take over a local shop she seized it and the first few weeks were bliss. Sure, they were stressful, but she was doing what she had always dreamed she would do and people really were loving her food.

The problem was that the blissful dream didn't really last. As is so often the case it turned into a nightmare and very quickly Dora was working 12-hour days six days a week. Dora was totally and utterly exhausted and on an hourly basis her profits would have worked out at less than the minimum wage.

The problem was that Dora just kept digging herself deeper and deeper into her work. Her comfort zone lay in making the food so she point blank refused to let anyone else be involved with its production. She would allow some of her staff to assemble the odd sandwich or to chop a few vegetables but beyond that it had to be her zone. She totally bought into the myth that she was the only one who could produce the great food. The more she buried her head in the kitchen though, the less time she had for the rest of the business. There was no time to be spent on marketing or tweaking the operational aspects of the coffee shop. Her staff drifted from table to table with no systems and the lunch-hour period in particular was complete chaos. It was loosely argued by some of her customers that this chaos was part of the charm of the business but that argument didn't hold quite so much sway for those customers who, visiting for the first time, had to endure a three quarters of an hour wait for a relatively simple lunch.

Everything in the business, almost without exception, was contained within Dora's head. Her little enterprise was almost completely devoid of systems. Her quarterly VAT returns passed in a haze of last minute calculator-bashing and a frantic scrabble to find the money to pay the bill. Her accounts would land on her frustrated accountant's desk the week before they were due and he, thinking he understood 'business', would keep telling her to put her prices up because she wasn't making enough money.

But that wasn't the solution. Dora needed to stand back and learn how to manage her business. She needed to work 'on' it rather than working *relentlessly 'in' it. And the only way for her to do that was to start putting in some systems, to train up some staff (or recruit new better ones) and to have a little trust that these people could do the job as well as she did.*

With many of our true stories we sometimes have to tweak and amend a few details to protect the client or business involved. This means that in some cases the actual client might not actually be aware that it is them we are talking about but for these two stories a slightly different pattern emerges. Dick will immediately recognise himself and his business but Dora might not. In an odd way though there are dozens of Doras who we have met over the years who will assume the story is about them. That is because Dora's story is so familiar and Dick's is so rare.

WEIGHING IT ALL UP AND TIPPING THE SCALES ONE WAY OR THE OTHER

Now you've heard both the good and bad sides of owning and running your own coffee shop – it's time to make your decision.

Whenever you see a successful business, someone once made a courageous decision.

Peter F. Drucker

So now what? What will you do?

WHAT DO YOU WANT TO DO FOR THE REST OF YOUR LIFE?

That's the big question here. That's pretty much what this is all about.

And if the answer really is 'run a little coffee shop' or 'open and build a chain of the world's best coffee shops', or even 'blow Starbucks out of the water', then that is what you really should do. Do that thing. At a really basic level that's the right thing to do. If this is really truly what you want to do then do it – if you don't, then don't.

All we want to emphasise is that the dream may not be what you had envisioned. It will, without a shadow of a doubt, involve a number of lows as well as highs so you cannot go into it unless you really want it and you have your eyes wide open. So how much do you really want this? How much will you work and focus and concentrate on doing the right things within your business? Or will you just get stuck 'in' the business and slog away gradually becoming more resentful of your customers, the economy, staff, tax officials, environmental health officers etc.

If you're focused enough and want to do it enough then let's go.

If not, put this book down, sell it on the Amazon marketplace, forget the dream and clock in again on Monday.

It's up to you.

Start with the end in mind

Clarity of mind means clarity of passion, too; this is why a great and clear mind loves ardently and sees distinctly what it loves.
Blaise Pascal

So you're still here? Good, well let's get on with it. But before we start there are a few more rules. It's incredibly easy to get carried away with enthusiasm and jump straight into your first business. We've done it many times. The inner Richard Branson in all of us thinks we can just get going and it'll all work out. Sadly, Branson has a huge team around him these days and a very clear idea of what he wants from each new venture. And like nearly every entrepreneur on the planet, he has learned this the hard way with a few unpleasant mistakes along the way – Virgin Cola anyone?

Starting with the end in mind is, without a shadow of a doubt, one of the key skills in business, and yet it is almost criminally ignored, particularly within the coffee shop industry. Once you have decided to get going you need to map out in intricate detail how your life will look in three, five or even ten years. The big mistake that most operators make is that they jump in quickly from the wrong perspective – they jump into the business because they want to get out of where they currently are and focus on the creation of a short term and unrealistic dream or vision of their lovely new coffee shop.

Habit two – Begin with the end in mind.
Stephen Covey, *The Seven Habits of Highly Effective People*

The correct way to do it is to imagine yourself several years down the line and see if you can create the vision of the lifestyle that you ideally want. Some of the key questions that you need to ask yourself are:

■ How many hours will you want to be working?

■ How many days a week will you work?

■ How much money would you like to earn each year?

■ How many weeks holidays do you want to take?

■ How long do you actually want to be doing this for?

■ What sort of money would you like to be able to sell the business for?

■ What will you do after you sell it?

■ Will you want your children to work in the business?

■ Will you be able to take a month or so off if necessary?

■ What will happen if you break a leg or fall ill?

■ Will you work hands-on in the business yourself?

■ Will you expand and open several sites?

These questions, which may seem slightly indulgent, are actually at least as important as where you locate your business or what sort of food you'll offer at lunch. But ignore them at your peril. If you don't have crystal clarity with these questions then you'll very quickly allow the business to control you. This will happen with alarming speed and before long you'll have created a business that simply won't meet those needs and desires because you'll have adopted an 'I'll just do this for a while' attitude for too long. You'll also find yourself swayed by the opinions of other business owners who will insist that your original goals are pure fantasy.

Don't create a trap for yourself

The harsh reality is that a business that involves you having to be there every hour of the day isn't a business at all. It's a trap. You've bought yourself a job which, regardless of what you may think, simply isn't the right thing to do. A business like this will also have very little value since it presents an unappealing option for anyone to buy.

One of the largest sections of our 'formula' is the systems section and that's for a reason. It's the biggest area that most new operators fall down on. The model you're after should always be the Dick model from the 'Good cop' section, and the model to avoid should be Dora from the 'Bad cop' section. So keep this etched in your mind whilst you're working and keep moving forward to this vision every day.

At the start of the business you will need to work very long hours and graft hard to deal with all the problems and hurdles you encounter, but as long as you keep your vision of the end goal in mind then that's okay. That becomes your driving force. You fix the problem with a view to never having it surface again, or if it does you'll have a system to deal with it. An operator without a clear end in mind won't do this – he or she will simply accept it as part of the business and keep fixing it every time it arises.

So get this end goal clear in your mind and stick to it. Write it down, keep referring to it and create a set of rules that are consistent with it.

Establishing clear rules of operation

The establishment of clear rules of operation will become vital in your business but initially these rules need to apply to you and how you conduct yourself and your time in the business. At this stage it's all possibility, so make sure you come up with something that really, truly fits in with what you want. That means not being swayed by those who think it isn't possible and also exposing yourself to lots of people who have managed to achieve success on their own terms. You need to read lots and lots of business biographies at this stage. This is vastly more useful than exposing yourself to a couple of bank managers or perhaps a friend or acquaintance who has slogged away, superficially successfully, for 40 years in their own business and seems keen to impart lots of 'you have to be there' advice.

You need to step up and gain some altitude over your business and concept so that you can have complete clarity. A great book to read, even though it is in a wildly different market, is Tim Ferriss' *The Four Hour Workweek* (Vermillon). In this book, Tim highlights exactly how he runs a hugely successful online business whilst travelling round the world and devoting around four hours a week to the business. This may not be your model or what you want to do but, if you want to craft something really great that doesn't control your life you must realise what is possible at this stage . In our own businesses we reached this stage many years ago and realised that a single and highly successful coffee shop could be managed on less than four hours a week – so please do not assume that this great 'four-hour workweek' model is something that can only apply to other businesses.

We'll say it again. It's your business, your model and it's up to you to create, from the very beginning, a model that suits you and your lifestyle.

Our Eureka moment

If you refer to Act II of the Johnny True Story in the systems section, you'll see how this was first applied to a fish and chip shop. This was a Eureka moment for both of us. Not just because it was the first proof that the creation of strong rules and a clear model that is laid out (in great detail) in advance actually can create a great business, but also because the highly systemised model allowed us lots of spare time to experiment with innovative techniques with marketing, and even things like the provision of exceptionally high quality coffee totally free for the customers – these are the sorts of things that a classic fish and chip shop owner would recoil at and regard as totally unacceptable because they are so totally mired in the day-to-day running of the business. It was our shop that, within 18 months of operation, was voted the best fish and chip shop in Ireland – and the proof is clearly in the (slightly greasy and fishy) pudding.

So what can these rules be?

Anything you really want is available within reason. If you accept that you'll have to work hard for the first few months (depending on how large your ambitions are), you can then set a date at three, six, twelve months (or even day one) that your rules will apply from. They can be things like:

- I will never work a shift behind the counter.
- I will ensure I have eight weeks holiday per year and take a month off in summer.

- I will work no more than three hours a week in the business.

- I will never miss any family event that is important to me.

- I will make £50,000 per year for ten hours work per week.

- My family is more important than my business and will always come first.

- I won't ever wear a tie again.

When creating your rules, don't get caught up with how they might work or allow 'well that could never happen, that's impossible' thoughts to come into your thinking. Create them with an open mind and then work to make sure they happen. For an example of these types of rules, go to the 'Coffee Boys Consulting' tab on our www.thecoffeeboys.com website. You'll see our rules there and they include a number of slightly fun things like 'no ties', 'have a laugh', as well as some pretty clear stuff about the way we charge and what we expect clients to do. In many cases this can be regarded as extreme arrogance, but let's make one thing crystal clear once more – it's up to you to set the rules. It's your business and you must craft it in a way that suits you. For our consulting business the same applies.

Now here's the strange thing. A business with extreme clarity of personal rules for the owner will always be a better business than one that doesn't have these rules. It almost doesn't matter how odd or arrogant these rules may appear to be – it's the clarity that helps craft the business and helps create something great. A consultancy business that has no rules and allows the client to dictate everything will always struggle, and a coffee shop that allows the customers and staff to dictate the operational structure will almost certainly be a painful and unprofitable experience at best and doomed to failure at worst.

**Our most successful clients always have strict rules of operation – even if they don't have them written down they permeate every aspect of the business.
So ignore Part One at your peril.**

Part Two

The Entrepreneur Skills Matrix

KEY LESSONS BEFORE YOU EVEN CONTEMPLATE POURING YOUR FIRST CUP OF COFFEE

If you've made it this far we have to assume that you haven't been put off. The good cop has won you over and you stood up manfully (or indeed womanfully – if such a thing exists) to the bad cop. You are, in short, ready for action. But just before we launch into your formula for success and you begin the actual process of opening your shiny new coffee shop, there are a number of really key skills that we have identified that you must have if this grand adventure isn't to become a horrible nightmare – perhaps like that recurring one you used to have as a child when you went to school only wearing your underwear.

But we've done all the bad cop stuff. You know the pitfalls of failure. So here are the key skills you'll need to avoid them. You'll notice (we hope) that not once does the ability to make a great cup of coffee appear on the list. At this stage there is a reason for that as will become clear.

KEY ENTREPRENEUR SKILL NUMBER ONE: RELENTLESS, PIG-HEADED DETERMINATION

All great, and indeed not so great, businesses start with a dream. They start with an idea of what the final business will look like. As you sit reading this you undoubtedly have a vision of how you want your customer treated, how the coffee will look, the quality of the buns, and, indeed, even the seemingly petty (but almost equally vital) importance of having clean toilets.

> *You have to learn the rules of the game. And then you have to play better than anyone else.*
>
> Albert Einstein

You'll have a vision of how it will all look. You'll possibly know the exact colour you want the walls to be. You'll know how you want the counter positioned because you feel that will work best for the customer as well as the staff. All these factors will constitute this great vision of the way you want the business to finally look.

The problem is that reality is about to bite you very, very hard. Long before you open the front door to the first customer, you are going to have to deal with a lot of incredibly annoying people. You'll meet landlords who tell you that they couldn't possibly allow you to have a ten-year lease when they only are offering five. You'll meet solicitors who tell you that under no circumstances will they be able to progress your legals because they are visiting Rupert and Cynthia at their new Tuscan farmhouse and that the 'other parties'' solicitor will be on holiday too. You'll meet builders who simply cannot bother their slightly exposed backsides to turn up on time and actually do one single thing that they promised to do. You'll stand like a totally naïve school child being bewildered by shop fitters who tell you all sorts of guff as to why your coffee machine couldn't possibly be plumbed in where you want it to be.

You'll meet uniform manufacturers who'll argue 'black is white' and that they didn't agree to the date that you have written down in your little book. You'll meet equipment suppliers who will tell you that the choice of the equipment you want really won't work properly and why don't you try their choice instead? (conveniently ignoring the detail that they get a kick-back from the manufacturer they recommend and not from the one you want). They'll tell you that the serve-over fridge will work fine in your shop when the reality is that it simply won't. They'll tell you that they have put together lots of businesses just like yours but conveniently ignore the fact that they have never operated one.

Sadly those 'meets' are the tip of a large iceberg and you're about to have your patience tested fairly relentlessly and extensively every day to see your vision through. The key throughout all of this is to digest all this new information as rationally as possible but to stick to your guns where necessary. Most of the time things are possible when you're told that they're not. Never forget that most of the people you are dealing with simply want an easy life. They just want to be able to get home as early as possible. They just want to do a 'good enough' job, so they don't get shouted at by their boss.

But you have chosen a different path, and to come up with this new and truly great business you're going to have to really knuckle down and not accept second best.

Even once you're open too it won't ease up. You'll still have to deal with staff who continually want things to shift their way. They'll want to play their own music, they'll want to be paid more than you want to pay them, they'll insist that customers keep asking for certain items when actually this simply isn't true but it just suits some agenda of their own (like making their job easier). You'll have to deal with highly manipulative staff who try to turn you against great staff. You will be continually bombarded with suggestions and input which will try to dilute the perfection that you are striving for.

Your job is to ignore all this and keep going. To keep striving for that vision and to not allow yourself to be knocked back. Of all the key skills this may well be the most important.

Johnny pig-headed: true story number one

I have a client who opened a quite staggering number of retail sites in one year at one stage in his business career. Dealing with more than one or two new sites every year is stressful in the extreme and fraught with relentless problems since you have so many individuals, such as planners, estate agents, landlords, builders and solicitors (on both sides), all of whom have different agendas.

This client, through quite remarkable levels of pig-headed determination managed to keep forging forward regardless of any problems he seemed to encounter with a unique, and possibly not entirely healthy, combination of humour and huge (but brief) temper losses. Through it all though he had a number of excellent turns of phrase that used to help put the situation in perspective.

I was working in a consultancy role for a new coffee bar outlet he was putting together and I sat in on a meeting with him and the design guy who was creating the graphics for the windows. There was a problem with how the graphics were going to be positioned. The design guy was proposing that we just put them outside the window but I have used this strategy before and very often if there are kids about, as there were at this site, they just get picked off and very quickly leave an unsightly and sticky mess.

The problem was that there was a wooden panel stuck to the lower inside half of the window which prevented the graphics from going on this side. The designer insisted that it was too difficult and that we would have to just put them outside and hope for the best.

My client leaned forward and with his usual mixture of humour and extreme assertiveness remarked:

'In 1969 we put a man on the moon. You're telling me that we can't put a ******* graphic on the inside of the window? I'll tell you how we'll do it', he smirked and changed his tone slightly, 'we'll take the panel off the window by unscrewing those screws, we'll put the graphic on and then what do you think we'll do? Yes – we'll put the panel back on again.'

Needless to say the message got through and without any further problems he got what he wanted. This attitude, and the 'In 1969 we put a man on the moon' line in particular have stuck with me and I'm ashamed to say I use it every time I'm confronted with this kind of 'we'll take the easy way out' mentality. I recently told another client the story and since he is undergoing rapid growth and expansion within his business he now uses the line with his own builders and anyone else he is working with.

It's a great line to keep in your head and I heartily recommend that you use it when you're encountering problems like that.

Johnny pig-headed determination: true story number two – because it's so important!

One of the key points of being a male is to rarely, if ever, give any praise to your friends or colleagues. To offer praise could be regarded as weakness and indeed, within the somewhat harsh Irish humour, leave you open for ridicule.

So it with some trepidation that I offer up a positive critique of Hugh's character. But it also illustrates why he is such a useful person to work with. Hugh has a variety of skills (and a vast number of flaws) but the one thing that stands above everything else is his relentless pig-headed determination.

At times this frustrates the life out of me. Relentlessly pig-headed people can be difficult to be around. They tend to never forget or gloss over deadlines, they keep badgering suppliers and work partners to produce results in a way that can often be awkward. They never decide that something is 'good enough' and they're extremely difficult to persuade to just 'go with the flow'.

But these people get things done. It's that characteristic that makes him incredibly useful to be around. While I'm losing focus and dreaming up grand new ideas Hugh pulls me back to the job in hand and pulls out one of his infernal project plans to keep me on track.

So if you're not going to be pig headed in your business you must have someone around you who will be. Trust me – it is the single most important skill for success.

KEY ENTREPRENEUR SKILL NUMBER TWO: TAKING COMPLETE AND UTTER RESPONSIBILITY FOR YOUR BUSINESS

This is a particularly harsh lesson to learn but once fully grasped creates an almost zen like state of control. One of the harsh realities (and some might say flaws) of current society is that we basically grow up in a state of expectation that there is someone else to blame. All the way through school we have little control over our lives and are increasingly allowed, and indeed even encouraged, to blame the system for any failures. As we move into adult life through universities or apprenticeships we also have a blanket of 'control' thrown over us. There is always a support structure to help.

Responsibility is the price of freedom.

Elbert Hubbard

In our working lives we have bosses and HR departments to help us out. We have a guaranteed minimum wage to make sure we're paid fairly and endless disciplinary and grievance procedures to help us out and tangle our bosses in red tape should we actually be rubbish at our jobs and deserve to be sacked.

Should, horror of all horrors, we actually be sacked, we then have a decent social security system to help support us and pay the rent and provide food for the table. We might stub our toe on a loose paving slab and that not only allows us to sue (at no risk – No Win No Fee!) the local authorities as well as having many years of disability allowance paid.

This sounds like a political and social rant, and to a large extent it is, but ignore the politics and look at how this structure actually creates people who are singularly ill-equipped to take responsibility for their lives. Not having that skill is a huge reason why so many businesses fail. They fail because there is always someone to blame and, more importantly, that blame will generally be accepted by our friends or family.

When your business fails it's very easy to blame the economy, greedy landlords, useless staff, ill-educated customers, terrorists, global credit crunch or any other factor that is conveniently hitting the newspapers at that time. But it's all nonsense . . .

You fail because you made poor decisions and didn't create a proper business structure to begin with.

That statement is highly contentious and you may well find yourself recoiling at it and mentally listing examples of friends or family who didn't fail through any fault of their own. It is a very hard concept to grasp but the mere fact that you open a business in the first place indicates that you are taking responsibility for that new entity. That's how you need to view it, and once you do fully grasp the concept it allows you to view every problem as something that you will methodically and systematically deal with – not something that you can moan about to your friends and family and then sit back and wait for the inevitable demise of your business.

Let's take a few specific complaints.

1. **Greedy landlords.** To a large extent a landlord can only charge as much as the market will bear. That sounds awfully idealistic but it is indeed fact. They cannot simply double your rent after you have moved in. So if you're paying a high rent it generally means that you are in a high-traffic or affluent area. This means that you need to reflect it in your prices. You need to get that extra few percent of turnover from these affluent people to cover that extra few percent of rent you're paying. You do not need to go bust and blame the landlord, however compelling that may seem at times.

2. **All staff are rubbish.** Total nonsense but an incredibly common excuse for business failure. The hiring, training and retaining of great staff is an absolutely crucial skill to develop (we'll deal with it extensively later) but it is one that is almost criminally lacking in many small coffee shop operators. Great staff do exist. It is your responsibility to find and hold onto them.
3. **Minimum wage.** Minimum wage applies across the board. We all have to deal with it, so deal with it! Again it may mean that prices creep up a fraction, but that's necessary because for too many years we simply haven't been paying people enough in hospitality, and therefore the customer has not been paying enough for the food and drink that they eat when they are out and about. The advantage is that jobs in coffee shops suddenly become comparable to jobs in other industries and this is a good thing i.e. you have a larger pool of people to recruit from.
4. **'The government'.** This catch-all term covers all manner of ills. Pick and choose whatever you want to fit it into your situation. Income taxes, sales taxes, environmental health officers, planners – whatever your problem is there is likely to be someone to blame in government. But again it's the same for everyone. Go in with your eyes wide open and accept that many businesses manage to operate perfectly successfully with lots of government interference. So can you if you just accept that it is simply part of running a busisness.
5. **'Starbucks'.** Starbucks (and indeed any large chain) is a fantastic example of a great excuse for a business closing down. Generally it can be muttered in a 'Oh you know Starbucks opened down the road and really how can I compete with them?' fashion. Expect sympathetic nodding and agreement from your friends. Starbucks is great to bash – it has become 'the man' to many people. A huge great big beast of an 'excuse' that all operators can use if times are tough. But here are the basic facts. Starbucks transformed the industry and allowed us ALL to charge vastly more for a cup of coffee and subsequently (in many countries) created this huge coffee shop opportunity in the first place! Likewise Starbucks is so large that there is enormous local advantage to be seized by simply *'not* being Starbucks'.

The list above needn't stop at five points. It actually needn't stop at 20 or even 100. The point is that you must go into this with the attitude that it fails or succeeds based on your efforts – not external factors. If you get hit by an earthquake in the first week then make sure you're properly insured and start up again. If you get shut down by environmental health, then it's your fault (even if it was your staff who created the issue) simply because YOU didn't put in the systems and procedures to make sure that everything operates properly.

It's tough to accept but is an incredibly key skill in terms of running any business, and a total understanding of the concept will make your chances of success exponentially better.

KEY ENTREPRENEUR SKILL NUMBER THREE: PROVIDE TONS OF VALUE

This seems like classic common sense but it really isn't. Trust us, day in and day out, we see the same penny pinching, petty attitude towards customers from operators – owners who feel that the best way to run their business is to squeeze every last penny out of the customer in every single sale. The key skill to getting customers to return to your coffee shop, and more importantly tell their friends about it, is to provide huge value.

'Provide tons of value' is a loose term but it should cover everything you do. It also has nothing to do with price. You may have the most expensive coffee in your town but it could still be amazing value simply because you do everything brilliantly. A delicious chocolate brownie for £1.95 will always provide better value than a revolting one at 50p. This attitude needs to pervade every pore of your business and you will need to drum it relentlessly into your staff. It's highly unlikely that they will have worked for someone with this attitude before, so you need to make sure that they completely grasp that everything you do is about creating outstanding value and not about making as much money in as short a period of time as possible. Real lasting money and profits only flow after lots of value has been created.

> *You don't get paid for the hour. You get paid for the value you bring to the hour.*
>
> Jim Rohn

The value concept extends beyond your product offering too though. To recruit and retain great staff you need to provide great value for them. They need to feel valued and feel like they are getting a lot more out of their job than just a pay check at the end of the week.

Customers and staff simply aren't used to getting lots of value, so real, over-the-top value helps create a great talking point. And when your staff start talking about you positively outside of work the job of getting new customers and recruiting great staff becomes an awful lot easier.

Johnny true story – The Formula One mindset and how you need to apply it to your business

Formula One racing has eternally fascinated me ever since I was a child. In my imagination I would run everywhere as a Formula One driver skidding perfectly round the corners of the corridors in my school. As I grew up I was intrigued about a few of the characters within the sport and gradually started to realise that the guys at the real pinnacle were those who actually worked harder than anyone else. In the early seventies, Jackie Stewart was the best. He won three world championships but equally he was the first driver to really push himself professionally and take standards to a new level. Later in the seventies, Niki Lauda won three championships and yet clearly in certain situations he wasn't necessarily the fastest driver. On the right day James Hunt had an obvious surfeit of talent over Lauda and yet he only won a single championship. I read two autobiographies of Lauda during my teens and became interested in how much he worked at improving himself and taking fitness to a new level. The fact that he managed to create a successful airline business too showed just how shrewd he was.

Into the eighties and Ayrton Senna started to dominate. Outwardly it was easy to regard him as an otherworldly talent, but again he was a champion who took fitness to an entirely new level. He helped create a team around him within Honda that was incredibly loyal and almost impenetrable to another team mate. One of the great myths and legends about Senna was his amazing skill in the wet. What is often forgotten is that as a child learning in karts he was rubbish in the wet. His first kart race on a wet circuit was a disaster.

Humiliated by this bad race he made sure that every time there was a drop of rain falling he would get the kart out and practise relentlessly. It drove him with a passion and as a result he was pretty much unbeatable as an adult in the wet in a Formula One car.

Michael Schumacher, winner of a quite staggering seven world championships, is another case in point. Undoubtedly possessing enormous talent he was also the hardest working driver on the pit and the fittest guy throughout his career. Success, as the motivational guys say 'leaves clues'.

But the really fascinating thing about Formula One is when you look at the business behind all the glamour. The speed of change and improvement is quite incredible. The expression that is always bandied around in Formula One is that 'if you're standing still you're falling behind'. Not a week goes past without relentless development of the cars and testing of new parts. Back at the base there will be an entire team working away on next year's car – pouring over every detail of the rules in an effort to try and find some competitive advantage.

The difference between a Formula One business and the average coffee shop is approximately the size of the Grand Canyon. Most coffee shops establish themselves and then maybe make a couple of tweaks a year to their menus or some other aspect of the business. The scale and size of the business is radically different but the mindset of constant change and development and relentless improvement just like in Formula One can help provide enormous competitive advantage in a coffee shop. Make sure you put this into your business from day one and ignore the sleepy practices of your competitors.

KEY ENTREPRENEUR SKILL NUMBER FOUR: REALISM – THE ABILITY TO REALLY SEE THINGS AS THEY ARE

Entrepreneurs are, by their very nature, dreamers. They have to be dreamers to initially come up with the great new concept that will revolutionise the industry. In your case this means that you are dreaming of doing a better job (hopefully far better) than the competition. This will become an all-consuming passion (which we'll deal with later) and this passion will launch you headlong into a signed lease and a number of slightly daunting chats with banks and accountants.

So the ability to dream and to dream big is a crucial skill to get yourself going, but it is also a serious drawback when you are actually operating your business. You must learn how to shift from dream mode into a hard grafting operations manager who will leave no stone unturned in the pursuit of perfection. The physical process of putting a dream into action is tough and it requires fairly relentless attention to detail.

You don't have to do it all yourself but you DO need to be totally realistic about how your vision and dream is panning out. If your products or service are not really all they could be, then you must act. You cannot continue to exist in a dreamland that 'next month' it will all be okay if you get a 'good manager'. See it as it really is and ACT.

KEY ENTREPRENEUR SKILL NUMBER FIVE: FINANCIAL DISCIPLINE

Sadly, this is the key skill that is lacking in most entrepreneurs. Again the skills of being a good accountant are radically different to the creative talents required to create a perfect cappuccino or a delicious chocolate brownie. But you cannot ignore the requirement for this skill or you will end up in a LOT of trouble very soon.

If you don't or can't get your head around the basic figures and financial rules that we outline in the finance section, then you must take responsibility for having someone in your business or close to you who will manage this. Every day we see operators who blindly carry on with terrible financials until they finally go bust. We know operators who have carried on for years with unprofitable businesses artificially propping them up with spouse's incomes or savings. In many cases these problems can be fixed in a matter of weeks.

Financial anxiety and suffering is enormously stressful as we both know from bitter personal experience and you must make sure that you avoid it at all costs.

Johnny true story – The man in the brown suit

One of the key factors in your marketing needs to be the development of a great and compelling story that helps your customers 'buy in' to what you do and your offer. We deal with this extensively later but here is my 'big' story. If you are a client and have ever seen me talk or have read any of my other books, it is highly likely that you know this story and for that I am totally unapologetic. The reason why I am unapologetic is that it is by far the most important learning experience I have encountered during my 20 years in business. Also it hopefully demonstrates to you the importance of keeping YOUR key story in front of your customers at all times so they can continue to understand why you work so hard at what you do.

The story relates to my sandwich and coffee bar business. After one of my partners went bankrupt and we discovered just what a huge mess the accounts were in we spent a period of time running round like headless chickens looking for finance. If you have a partnership and one partner becomes bankrupt by law all financing that applies to all partners must cease and be re-negotiated. It makes sense since the whole point of being bankrupt is to draw a line under the current situation and stop all credit to the bankrupt party.

Of course this caused myself and my other partner (there were three of us in total) a huge headache. Overnight all loans, overdrafts and our factoring process (by which we were able to fund the slow payments within our sandwich distribution business) ceased. It all literally stopped and we were left having to find somewhere in the region of £100,000 instantly, and all monies due from our own debtors (the people who owed us money) had to be paid straight to the bank and not to our account.

With 60 employees being paid on a weekly basis and weekly accounts with most of our various product suppliers, it would be an understatement to say this caused a little financial pressure.

But we had a number of key advantages in our favour. Our sandwich and coffee bars (as opposed to the sandwich factory) were actually making money. We didn't know how much, but they were all cash positive and cash meant cash, i.e. at the end of the day there was cash in the tills that could be mopped up and spread thinly around to keep us going.

Secondly, we had a great name. To a certain extent we were the golden boys in the Belfast area at that stage and our brand was very strong. It was something that potential investors as well as customers would want to buy into.

But, and it's a BIG but, our financials were a complete mess. The bankrupt partner (kicked out of the business at this stage) had acted as our accountant and it was incredibly difficult to decipher exactly where we were. This, coupled with the fact that the accounts produced by our external accountants were a year and a half out of date meant that it was extremely difficult for any potential investor to get a clear grasp on what they might be investing in.

One day I received a call from a friend who had recently recovered from a relatively similar situation. He had a basically successful business but on an underlying basis was doing all sorts of stuff that was making him no money at all. He hadn't the faintest idea where he was financially and seemed to have very little (i.e. nothing) to show for his efforts in the bank.

He had been helped however by an old family friend who was a very successful business man. This man had invested a little money in the business, but more importantly, had put in place some very strict financial controls. My friend suggested to me that he set up a meeting between all of us. With nothing to lose we readily agreed.

When the day came we tidied up the office and made sure there was plenty of fresh coffee. All the admin girls looked highly efficient and the factory was spotless and churning out sandwiches in a superficial air of calm and control should he want to have a look around. At the allocated time a huge Mercedes Benz S500 pulled up outside. In my mind some form of Donald Trump character was going to step out but instead out came a rather unassuming older man in a brown suit with a cigarette clamped between his teeth. We ushered him into the office and without any form of normal pleasantries, and declining coffee, he asked us simply:

'Okay boys – let's see where we are. How much money did you make last week?'

We paused. My business partner looked at me and I spluttered out some nonsense about how we couldn't possibly know that. We had four shops and a factory for goodness sake – there was no way we could know our profit weekly. Inwardly I thought 'what an idiot! Does he not know the size of our operation? Weekly profit and loss? What the hell was he talking about? No business could operate like that.'

He looked slowly at me and started to hunt around in his pocket. 'What do you mean you can't work out your profit for a week? I have a big café over in Bangor and this is what I do . . .'

He found what he was looking for in his pocket and pulled out an old brown envelope. The cigarette hung from his mouth with the ash forming a drooping arc at the end. On the brown envelope he started to write with a cheap Bic biro. 'At the start of the week I count all the stock in the shop. Everything. Every single thing. Every tea bag, every sugar cube and every single item of food. And then do you know what I do?'

We again glanced at each other and I muttered 'Errr. No.'

I record what I buy every day and record my sales every day. At the end of the week I count up all the wages and recount the stock. So what do you think I have then?'

To be honest I wasn't entirely sure. I mentally pictured a profit and loss in my mind and tried to work out what you would call what he had produced. He had left so many things out that it didn't really have a name. Certainly no name that I had been taught at university when we were studying profit and loss. What about the accruals, pre-payments, rent rates and all the other costs of a weeks trading? I muttered vaguely that I didn't know what he had. A meaningless brown envelope perhaps?

'I have my profit. I just take off the rent and a few other things and I have my profit. Every week. Every single week. I count at the start, count at the end and record during the week. Now is that hard?'

'No, well, I suppose not.' I spluttered. I didn't really know how to react to this. Business simply wasn't as simple as that. I was, however, aware of the irony of me thinking that whilst teetering on the edge of bankruptcy and this little man had clearly managed to make a huge fortune with these simple theories. I felt a bit like an uneducated idiot and wanted to try and reassert myself back into the situation. He certainly wasn't going to invest in us if he felt we were idiots. 'But what about depreciation? And accruals and all the energy costs?'

'Forget 'em. They don't matter for this.' He replied holding me with a steely glare. 'I can include them afterwards. These are your fundamentals. These businesses are simple but you gotta know your fundamentals. This is how it works. You pay X for your food, Y for your wages and what's left is your profit contribution. Do that and we'll know where you are. Now, will you do that for me?'

'Okay,' I mumbled. But I knew I wouldn't, and I think he knew it too. We could never do that for all our shops and the factory. It just wasn't possible. It would take too much time and anyway, so I thought, the figure would be too vague and therefore meaningless. But I was wrong.

With that he got up, handed me the brown envelope covered with his scrawls and jumped into his Mercedes. He had a plane to catch to Manchester where apparently he owned an office block. I owned a few blocks of Lego.

A week later he returned as promised and asked for the figures. We mumbled and spluttered about how we had been too busy trying to save the business. He fixed me with the coldest stare I think I've ever seen, wished us luck and left. I never saw him again.

Somewhere deep inside though I knew it had been a profound meeting. I was a long way from learning my lesson and it was just one meeting with a long string of investors who could potentially save us but it was unique in its simplicity and straightforwardness.

Two weeks later we closed the doors of the factory. We were unable to meet our creditors and had to lay off all 30 staff who worked there. We sold the shops for a fraction of their true value and managed to scrabble just enough money to stop ourselves from going bankrupt.

So it was a harsh lesson. A lesson that was particularly severe since we discovered later that during that period we had actually been making approximately £8,000 profit a month. With a small cash injection we could easily have saved the business. If only we had proved these basic fundamentals at the time to our friend with the brown suit.

KEY ENTREPRENEURIAL SKILL NUMBER SIX: THE ABILITY TO MAKE TOUGH DECISIONS AND 'NOT CARE WHAT OTHERS THINK'

The growth and success of your business and the creation of your own dream lifestyle will ultimately have more to do with your ability to 'get things done' by other people than by any innate talent you have for making great coffee. In the early stages you are extremely likely to fall into the trap of 'wanting to be liked' by your staff. You're probably going to be working alongside them on a daily basis and undoubtedly life will be more pleasant if you're 'all part of the team'. To an extent this is true, but do not forget that your staff are highly unlikely to be viewing working in your business as a long-term career move. You are betting your entire future, possibly your house and maybe even your sanity on this new venture – they are probably just looking for a 'nice wee job' or something to make them a bit of money before they go off travelling round the world for a year.

Success also requires the courage to risk disapproval. Most independent thought, new ideas, or endeavors beyond the common measure are greeted with disapproval, ranging from skepticism and ridicule to violent outrage. To persevere in anything exceptional requires inner strength and the unshakable conviction that you are right.

Chin-Ning Chu, *Thick Face Black Heart*

The point is that you cannot fall into the trap of simply being 'one of the gang'. You will have some very clearly defined goals for the business, and once you open these will be attacked on every front. If you persist in wanting to be liked by your team you will end up with a heavily watered down version of what you were originally trying to put together. You must practise making tough decisions on a daily basis to keep that ultimate goal and dream a reality. On our travels around the country we see a tremendous amount of operators who fall into the trap of letting their staff simply walk all over them, which is ultimately an incredibly debilitating trait both personally and for the business. They labour under the misapprehension that employees need to 'like you' before they will do anything for you. This is simply not true.

Johnny true story

I have a close friend who has an incredibly pressurised and important job. He has approximately 1,000 employees under his control and by the nature of the business they are often in extremely difficult situations. I was discussing how he managed these situations and how he had managed to advance his career so quickly. At this stage I had approximately 120 employees in my own business and was struggling with the day-to-day managing and developing of these people. The concept of dealing with nearly ten times as many was extremely daunting.

He joked about his inability to use a computer properly and the fact that many aspects of his 'skill-set' were completely lacking. In fact in a very self-deprecating way he said that actually he only had one skill. And what was that skill:

The Ability To Get Other People To Do Things

That's all. He had carved out this great career simply by being able to 'get stuff done' by other people. This involved a tremendous amount of extremely tough decisions – the like of which you will never encounter in your coffee business. It involved him concentrating 100% on the goal and completely dismissing arbitrary notions of whether he would be liked or not as a result of his decisions.

It's easy to overlook the importance of this, especially when you are starting out and fuelled with your own self-importance and abilities in certain areas, such as coffee making or baking. But if you don't quickly grasp how to manage people properly then you are going to create a nightmare for yourself.

KEY ENTREPRENEURIAL SKILL NUMBER SEVEN: CRYSTAL CLARITY

The number one mistake that most inexperienced managers and owners make is a fundamental lack of clarity when communicating with staff. To a large extent this is a result of the industry having a lot of young and poorly trained managers who are put in positions of responsibility simply because they've been good at turning up on time for six months or so. What this results in is lots of young managers who haven't the faintest idea how to manage people. Subsequently, this means that there are lots of employees running around without the faintest idea of what is expected of them and what they should be doing.

Unfortunately this is something that both of us had to learn ourselves and that will clearly be the case for anyone who has successfully managed people. To begin with the tendency is to use almost apologetic language when asking people to do something for you or outlining the reasons why the shop needs to be run in a certain way. Coupled with weak body language and a slightly mumbling tone the message rarely gets through. This results in faint bleating from the young manager along the lines of: 'But I told her to do it', or 'They just never listen to me'.

Whoever knows he is deep, strives for clarity; whoever would like to appear deep to the crowd, strives for obscurity. For the crowd considers anything deep if only it cannot see to the bottom: the crowd is so timid and afraid of going into the water.

Friedrich Nietzsche

The ability to speak with crystal clarity about your objectives takes a little time and practice but certainly isn't rocket science. It involves getting the goal or objective crystal clear in your own mind and then choosing the right moment to articulate this. You need to speak confidently, hold eye contact and use completely unambiguous language. We do a lot of manager training within our business but ultimately it boils down to those key messages.

So the solution is to be crystal clear in all your communication. Forget the embarrassment of 'being a boss' and outline what you want to happen in words of one syllable. And then follow up. Again. And again. Until it has been done properly.

Hugo true story

In 2000, we were at a crossroads in our business. We had lots going on and we were involved in what we thought were all the areas and market sectors of the business that everybody else was involved in. We were 'all things to all men' as the phrase goes. Unfortunately we were also operating in a large degree of disarray – constantly firefighting situations and prioritising the urgent and important issues on a day-to-day basis. It was very chaotic and while good fun was becoming increasingly draining to all of us.

The first ever Speciality Coffee Association of Europe conference was being held in Monte Carlo and myself and the other two key people in the business decided to attend as a bit of a junket after a hard year. We also hoped it would give us the opportunity to take time out to discuss where we were going. We billed it as a strategy weekend – our very own annual conference and brainstorming event just like the big companies. On arrival the rain started (and didn't stop for three solid days) and we adjourned to a bar where we debated very candidly where we thought we were going wrong. Eight hours later we had agreed that the biggest problem was clarity. We didn't know what our end in mind was and we didn't spend enough time on planning – we just executed and as a result wasted so much time and energy with little measurement.

Our mantra for the weekend became crystal as in 'crystal clear' and we used that to benchmark nearly every part of the business over the next few days. In a lengthy, informal and brilliant conversation the three of us stuck together and kept our focus on developing and debating the issues. It became an effective milestone and mission for the subsequent years and it subsequently helped enormously with motivation, performance, effectiveness, profit and stress levels. Very soon everybody knew what our new objective was and we kept Crystal Clarity as our mantra for the business.

I am not suggesting that you need to go drinking for eight hours or travel to Monte Carlo (makes us sound rather grand actually) to achieve something similar. I do however strongly recommend that you get your key people offside in a relaxed environment for an extended period to allow for some frank and lengthy exchanges. Everybody needs to have the opportunity to feel heard and the discussion can be developed in a way that is almost impossible in the normal busy and time starved playing field that you operate in. This could transform your business. It builds trust and develops relationships. We all know that a business is about people so the people need to have some fun from time to time. It is well worth the cost even for small businesses like mine – just keep them out of the casinos!

Part Three

The Great Formula!

HOW WE DEVELOPED THE GREAT FORMULA

The Great formula was developed after a pretty exhaustive process of trying to work out what separated the folk who succeeded from those who didn't. In today's immediate gratification-obsessed society it would be wonderful to think that there is one key 'secret' to success in this business (or indeed in life). The quite staggering success of the movie and book *The Secret* (where the basic premise is that you simply have to focus and want something enough for it to miraculously appear) shows that people are crying out for easy options.

> *Being busy does not always mean real work. The object of all work is production or accomplishment and to either of these ends there must be forethought, system, planning, intelligence, and honest purpose, as well as perspiration. Seeming to do is not doing.*
>
> Thomas A. Edison

Unfortunately, in our ever-humble opinion, life and more specifically the creation and management of a great coffee bar isn't that easy. But there is a formula or road map that can help to point you in the right way. There are, without a shadow of a doubt, a set of characteristics that are common to the great businesses and generally the unsuccessful ones are simply lacking one or two of the key parts of the formula. From our perspective, when we are analysing businesses for clients it becomes a relatively simple process of highlighting what is missing (usually apparent within the first few minutes of contact) and then going through the occasionally arduous task of filling the gap. The difficulty normally arises not in creating the strategy but in persuading the owner or operator that the specific problem in their business is a relatively simple thing that they have simply ignored.

THE BASIC FORMULA

The basic formula is as follows.

Passion creates great taste (for both food and drink) which is then positioned correctly in the market to the right customers. Great people are recruited to help run the business and they in turn provide great service to the great people who we call customers. This great product served by great people then needs to be correctly marketed and a system needs to be applied to the business to help ensure that it works in a relatively seamless fashion, regardless of whether the owner is present or not. Finally (and this is generally the hardest point of all to get across), the business needs to focus very hard on the creation of money – a profit.

We will go into these seven key parts of the formula in greater detail in the coming sections, but initially we want to show you what happens when you leave out just one key part. The Great Formula flowchart (Figure 1) attempts to illustrate exactly what happens when some of these key parts of the formula are ignored by coffee shop owners.

Coffee shop owner number one

The top line illustrates the perfect coffee shop, the owner of which has correctly applied the formula. They arrive at the end of the line with SUCCESS. The smug owner can comfortably lie on the beach outside their holiday home in the South of France without a constant gnawing state of panic about the chaos that may be happening at home or the increasingly precarious state of their finances.

Coffee shop owner number two

Coffee shop owner number two has bravely escaped the rat race but has ignored the second crucial stage of the formula, i.e they have neglected the passion. We'll go into this later, but a business without passion is generally doomed to a mediocre offer and has no inherent and unstoppable drive for excellence of product. Without a passionate vision of how the business is going to do something great you ultimately end up with something that doesn't quite work and has low sales.

Coffee shop owner number three

Our third intrepid coffee shop owner has the passion but simply hasn't allowed this passion to correctly translate into great sales. They have been worn down by

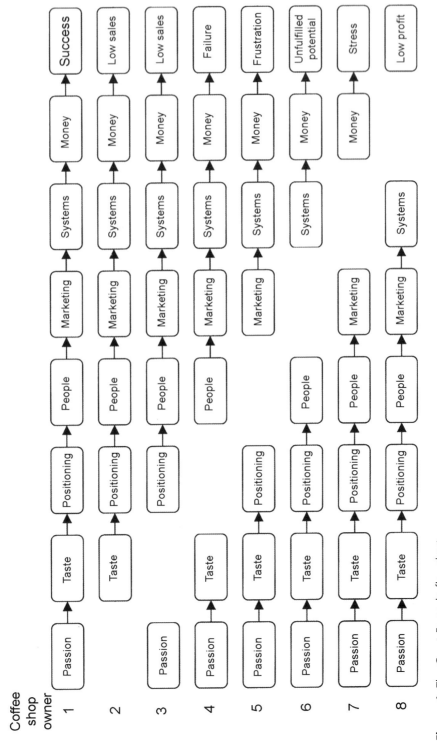

Figure 1. The Great Formula flowchart

all those suppliers or staff who tell them that their vision simply isn't workable in the real world. They haven't had the pig headed determination to see things through properly and force through their agenda. The net result of this is a business that will simply plod along with low sales from a mediocre offer. If they get the rest of the formula right they may well survive (although it is by no means guaranteed) but the business will never be the resounding success that the owner originally imagined.

Coffee shop owner number four

The fourth brave soul to open has neglected to properly position their business within the market. They have rushed headlong into the dream and passionately created a wonderful product. Sadly though, they simply don't have a market for it. They have produced the equivalent of a builder's café in an affluent shopping area or a fancy patisserie by the docks. Sometimes it simply doesn't matter how good your product is – if you don't have a market for it, ultimately your business will, unless you substantially change the offer, be doomed to failure.

Coffee shop owner number five

Our fifth nervous entrepreneur has correctly followed the first three steps but has then ignored the people side of things. He or she may have accepted that age old (and utterly false) wisdom that 'you have to do it yourself' and are standing frazzled and totally incapable of moving forward. Or they may have made a few cursory job hires and expected that these bright new starts would simply absorb what needed to be done by standing in close proximity to them. The final mistake they may have made is that they chose to ignore the fact that their customers were looking for a lot more than a great product and delivered pretty woeful customer service. This business is doomed to a lifetime of frustration and relentless blaming, i.e. taking the view that 'customers are idiots' or that 'it's impossible to get good staff these days'. The 'it's impossible to get good staff today' folk are the people that we see most often within our travels. They are always wrong.

Coffee shop owner number six

Our sixth exasperated owner has the first four boxes checked but sits patiently waiting every day for the customers to arrive. They simply cannot grasp why their competitors in the next road are so much busier than them. The only thing that they're certain of is that to market their product is tacky and would make them 'look desperate', which is ironic because desperation is exactly what they feel as they stare at the ceiling every night at 3.00 a.m. wishing they were back in their nice safe bank job.

Coffee shop owner number seven

Our seventh stressed friend is nervously sucking his blood pressure tablets as he pores over every fine detail of his business. Superficially everything is going well but he hasn't had a holiday in the past three years and is wondering whether 100-hour weeks was exactly what he had envisaged when he first decided to make the big move. There isn't a clear system anywhere in the business and why should there be? Everything is neatly stored in his head and since he's always working on site there seems little need to write it down.

Coffee shop owner number eight

Finally, entrepreneur number eight has ticked every one of the first six parts of the formula and he has a vibrant and superficially highly successful business. The only problem is that it doesn't really make very much money. At the end of every year he calculates that he has earned something similar to the minimum wage, but that's okay. He wasn't in it for the money anyway and as long as he keeps the customer's happy that's all that matters to him. A holiday somewhere other than Bognor might be nice though, and he spends a fair bit of time every quarter scrabbling around like a madman looking for his VAT payments.

So the lesson is – ignore the formula at your peril.

Coffee shop chains

With larger businesses though we tend to see a slightly different problem emerge. What we find is that when putting together coffee bar operations for larger companies, who already have a management structure in place, we discover one final and ultimately life threatening problem. Slow, painful, incredibly frustrating death by concept dilution.

CONCEPT DILUTION

Concept dilution occurs when too many people try to have a say in how the business grows and evolves. This can take a wide variety of formats and in many cases is well-meaning. It is incredibly destructive though because the growth and development of a chain of coffee bars involves an incredibly strict adherence to the basic initial premise (and passion) that created it. Because the passion within a larger and more obviously commercial business is, almost by definition, driven by profit, you constantly struggle with various interested bodies trying to change and amend the vison to make things more efficient or cut costs.

The difficult thing is that a young business DOES require incredible flexibility and a need to change and amend the offer within the first couple of years, but those decisions can only be taken by an incredibly driven entrepreneurial character or by people who really understand how to grow a business like this.

The sorts of people who must generally be avoided at all costs within the first couple of years are:

Accountants or financial controllers

This may appear to totally contradict our mantra that 'it's all about the money', but it doesn't. The harsh reality is that the type of character that is comfortable devoting their life to accountancy is about as far removed from the classic entrepreneur as it is possible to be. The accountant will always be wanting to drive down costs and will, for example, never fully understand why a wage bill needs to be a few percent higher than other existing businesses within the portfolio in the initial stages to ensure the customer gets a great experience even with relatively untrained staff. They will also find designer charges and initial marketing spend to be outrageous within their normal scheme of operation.

The problem is that if the accountant has too strong a hold on the ultimate decision maker, then he can easily sway their opinion too soon about the ultimate chances of success of the enterprise.

Buyers

Buyers have basically one job – to buy 'stuff' as cheaply as possible. They can go under various guises within different businesses but all your hard work nurturing great suppliers over the years and building up fantastic 'give and take' relationships can be dashed in one fell swoop by some over zealous buyer on the phone demanding an immediate 5% reduction across the board in prices. Likewise our buyer will have little or no concept of the difference between two types of coffee bean or machine and will simply see the coffee as a commodity and the more expensive machine as an ego driven indulgence.

A buyer may also force you to use different catering equipment suppliers or shop fitters or various other suppliers that help you to physically set the business up.

The problem with this is you generally have worked very closely with your own pet suppliers, and when the time comes for pig headed determination to be applied to a shop fitter or the catering equipment supplier, they know the standards you are prepared to work with. A supplier who you have no relationship with and who has been screwed to the floor with price, will have absolutely no interest in your bleating cries that the chilled cabinet that has been put in simply won't do because the curve isn't quite right and clashes with the rest of the design.

Buyers are a potentially huge minefield so beware.

Efficiency driven operational managers

These are another potential highly frustrating part of the big company mix. These are the folk who like to think they can 'kick arse' and get things done. They love to feel they can tweak and amend the offer to make it profitable by driving down wage bills, changing food suppliers at will, bullying staff to work long hours, and generally destroying the fine balance of great products, excellent service and a beautiful environment that you have slaved so hard to produce.

Operations managers are essential, but it should always be remembered that they are part of a delicate mix. Give them too much power and you'll see a great initial idea turn into a flawed and doomed concept within a very short period of time. This we have seen on more than one occasion.

Wives/husbands/friends/significant others of key people

At every level of a business it is quite staggering how often you have to deal with this issue. When setting up your own first site you will find an almost consistent bombardment of ideas coming through from people who quite frankly haven't got the faintest idea what they're talking about. The issue lies in the old banana that everyone feels qualified to run a coffee shop since they all visit them. What this means in a single-site start up is that you'll hear fairly often things like 'I went to the new (insert brand) café and they have these wonderful bacon rolls – you should do that . . .'. This uninformed opinion takes no account of your positioning, your planning use in terms of hot food, or even the way that you have structured your existing food offerings to cope with the flows of people at different times of day (see 'Taste' section).

At the larger business level it becomes even more infuriating when you are asked to consider comments such as 'The MD's wife suggested that you sell a range of coffee cakes because they seem to sell very well at her local coffee shop'. When you hear a line like this you are then forced to all sit round, keep a relatively straight face, and explain in a pleasant manner why this is utter nonsense and the MD's wife would be far better occupied actually doing something constructive rather than buying shoes and dreaming up daft notions in coffee shops with her friends before she toddles off for a half-hearted session with Bruce the personal trainer. Again though, you should be very aware just how much sway she can have around the dinner table at night.

The absolute pinnacle of 'smash your head on the table' frustration is when you hear that the director's daughter or son has come up with a great idea based on a 'cute muffin' they saw in a local shop. Or perhaps they have decided that everything should be organic/fair trade/locally sourced/ethical/green and why on earth doesn't Daddy's new business do that? Some time, if you catch us in a bar after a conference we can elaborate on these examples. Expect to hear some shouting though.

UNDERSTANDING HOW CONCEPT DILUTION MANIFESTS ITSELF

What happens is that your delicate initial model gets what we call 'picked at'. The various characters who want to stick their nose in will strongly argue that their individual decisions will actually make little difference to the ultimate model. But the problem is that in the initial stages of any new business you simply never get everything right. If a perfect business is an abitary 100%, then for the first few months you can expect no better than 90% of perfection, almost no matter how hard you work. There is always a period of bedding in with new staff, suppliers and the physical unit itself that will create a few tears and a fair amount of very late nights dreaming up solutions to your early problems. But 90% is okay. As long as you accept that it is 90% and isolate the constituent parts of the other 10% and then work really hard to make it better, you'll get through.

If you allow the concept diluters to come in with their pragmatic ways and 'common sense' (or indeed total utter nonsense) they can quickly pick a few extra percent off between them. Before you know it they have picked away the concept to maybe 75% of the original vision. And that's when the problems start. The simple fact is that 75% of a concept, no matter how great it may initially have been, is generally a pretty mediocre end result. And the chances of a mediocre business succeeding and growing rapidly into a great one are slim at best.

So avoid the concept diluters. They exist all around you and are actually present in small businesses too. And, as ever, the key skill is to stick to your vision and strap on the pig headed determination mask. These folk are exhausting to deal with and will, unless you are very strong, wear you down.

Part Four
The Great Formula Explained

1 Passion

This is the key starting point. You must have passion for producing a great product with great service.

There are lots of true stories of businesses that have had great successes through passionate owners and also lots of stories of people who simply didn't get the passion concept and thought that running a coffee shop was 'easy money'.

> *I love to play golf, and that's my arena. And you can characterize it and describe it however you want, but I have a love and a passion for getting that ball in the hole and beating those guys.*
>
> Tiger Woods

There is a wonderful supposedly true story about the opening of Disney World in Florida. This had been Walt Disney's great vision for many years and it was only through epic levels of pig headed determination by both Walt and his brother Roy that they managed to see it through. Sadly, Walt passed away before the opening and a journalist remarked to Roy that it was terribly sad that Walt had never lived to see what he had created. Roy replied 'Oh, Walt saw it. You're seeing it now because he saw it years ago.'

Walt Disney was a truly fascinating man. For many when he was proposing some of his hair-brained schemes, he was nothing more than a dreamer. Dreamers are looked down upon by many people as having no real grasp of reality. In many cases they do crash and burn, but equally often they are ground down by others so that they never fulfil their dreams. Many 'dreamers' spend their whole lives never taking the risk of actually making the brave leap and acting on their dreams, and this is a terrible shame.

Sadly, many of those who do act never fully put their dream into place because it's not backed up by a burning passion and a clear vision of EXACTLY what they want. Coffee shops (and restaurants) are probably the most dream-driven businesses out there. They are the types of business that huge swathes of people feel they are qualified to do and regard as a 'dream job'. The reality as they quickly find out is somewhat different. A recent survey by a UK women's magazine discovered that the top two dream jobs for women were:

1. Becoming a published author. The classic JK Rowling dream. Come up with a grand idea on a train and then write the first books from the heat of your local coffee shop. Make several hundred million pounds.

2. Set up a coffee shop or restaurant. Put all that dinner party skill into action and breeze in and out every day shaking a few hands and enjoying the 'huge profits' that are clearly available from a cup of coffee.

This survey tends to highlight just how much of a problem there is within the industry and why so many people plunge headlong into an extended mortgage and towards potential bankruptcy with nothing more than a good muffin recipe and a half decent location. The budding novelist rarely gives up their job to write the 'next Harry Potter' and their financial investment is little more than a large pile of envelopes and stamps to send the completed manuscript off to potential agents and publishers.

The difference between a Walt Disney and the majority of coffee shop entrepreneurs appears subtle but is in reality incredibly crucial. Disney had an incredibly clear vision of exactly what he wanted and this was driven by intense passion. Dreaming is a very different thing. For a dreamer to succeed they must turn this dream into a vision. Only the relentless clarity of a vision will keep driving the business forward and effortlessly batter Mervyn the salesmen (see page 60) out of the way as he and other dream-stealers inevitably appear.

But it all starts with passion. It's the passion that fuels the vision. If there is no passion for the perfectly extracted espresso or the world's most delicious chocolate brownie then you pretty much have a business doomed to failure from the beginning. So how does this passion manifest itself? Well we like to think that it can be tested with the 'food hall' test.

THE SHOPPING CENTRE 'FOOD HALL' TEST

One of the key tests we recommend is to walk through a local food hall in a busy shopping centre and judge what your reaction is. Don't pick one of the very new slick ones in an affluent area, but instead choose a normal centre that has been going for a few years. As you wander round what do you feel?

- Do you think that all those chains are doing a good job?

- Does their food or coffee look delicious?

- Do the staff look vibrant and excited to be there?

- Do you think their food looks fresh and appears to have been created with great care?

If your answers don't border on anger and outrage then you may well not actually care enough about what you're thinking of doing. To a large extent you need to be an incredibly annoying person to be with when you visit these types of places. You need to wander round indignantly shouting, ranting and annoying your spouse or friends with your total bewilderment at how these operations are still in business. You need to get so cross that you lie in bed at night and stare at the ceiling thinking 'Why? Why do people actually eat or drink that crap?'. You need to feel, to quote legendary chef and write Anthony Bourdain, that these places produce 'a terrible sameness and a lowering of expectations'.

Without this level of anger and disbelief at the competition you'll never create the vision to produce something better.

So why *are* you doing this? What *is* your passion? What is the driving force that will make you shape your vision? What is the image of *your* Disney world that you can see so clearly? An image that will keep you awake at night and will be powerful enough to keep you going as you encounter all the obstacles that will surely come in your way.

The reality is that very often people who start coffee shops aren't driven by this kind of passion and that makes it incredibly difficult for us to help them either to open or, more often, to help them out of the horrible anodyne mess they have created for themselves. We generally find that the people who start up coffee shops fall into four main camps.

1. **Folk who have obsessed and dreamt about the idea of setting up a coffee shop for many years**

   In idle moments as they sit in their job in the bank or make a batch of cookies at home, they let their thoughts drift to an idyllic notion of serving great customers with great food and living a care-free life. No boss. Nobody to tell them what to do on a Monday morning or check they have their weekly reports in on a Friday.

The dream festers and is increasingly reinforced by friends and family who tell them that their muffins or scones are much better than those served by Frank's Cakes down the road. Or they have a dinner party and the guests rant and rave about the food and insist it's better than they've had in any number of restaurants recently.

Eventually a situation will arise where they click into action. Perhaps they'll be made redundant or simply become fed up with their boss. They'll realise there is a large amount of equity in their house, or maybe they'll be left some money from an aunt or grandmother – enough money for the dream to kick in.

These people, even though they generally do pass the passion test, are usually the least likely to succeed. That's not to say they cannot on occasion actually do very well, but it will nearly always be too huge a learning curve and the dream will be quickly shattered.

2. People who currently work within the food side of the industry

These are generally chefs, bakers or self-trained cooks. They almost certainly pass the passion test but their perspective is driven almost entirely from the kitchen and the food side of things. Unfortunately, whilst this is very beneficial in many ways, it creates huge gaps in their ability to run the business. They tend to have been weaned on a diet of ranting 'Gordon Ramsay-style' behaviour and feel that as long as what they can produce tastes great that is all that matters.

They have generally got a decent grasp of food margins (usually having learnt the hard way or from an experienced food service boss) but again this is not always the case. A few of these characters still live under the illusion that great food will inevitably make good money and that previous bosses were too greedy in what they charged or were too focused on margins when great food should be more of an art. If they fall into the latter camp their demise will be swift and painful.

If they do grasp food margins and great food as a concept then that is only half the battle. Often they will tend to ignore the importance of truly great coffee and see it as a commodity that is of secondary importance to the food. They will veer towards fully automatic machines and buy on price rather than quality.

They also tend to have very little grasp of the mechanics of great customer service and the importance of the 'front of house', i.e. everything that happens in full view of the customer! A coffee shop needs at least as much emphasis on front of house as it does on the quality of food and drink that is served.

3. **People who work within the industry from the coffee side (generally, but not exclusively, these are baristas)**

Somewhat like the chefs, this group can be very blinkered about what exactly it is that a coffee shop needs to provide. The barista community is incredibly passionate and, at times, prepared to go into quite ludicrous levels of detail to produce the perfect shot of coffee. This passion is hugely beneficial because great passion helps to keep driving forward a great business and can tend to help bull doze obstacles in its way.

The other great advantage of baristas is that they are generally used to being customer facing – whether they like it or not (and many of them don't). They aren't shut away in a kitchen, like a chef. A good barista tends to be quite remarkably passionate about coffee but will often be very narrow in their focus and have a limited general understanding of the rest of the business.

Somewhat like a chef they tend to think that as long as they create great coffee the customers will swarm their shop. Sometimes this can actually be the case. In a cheap side-street location with low overheads there is a niche for serving outstanding coffee and almost ignoring many of the other issues. Great coffee can tend to attract other baristas who want to be part of the shop and as long as it's kept vaguely clean and the staff aren't too rude to the customers, the model can work quite well.

Where it falls down is when the barista simply ignores some of the basic economics of the business. Coffee sales alone will not pay the rent on a high street location. Somebody still has to handle hiring and firing staff and dealing with outside agents like accountants and environmental health officers. Somebody needs to sit down every so often and work out if they're actually making money. Somebody has to sit down and write a cheque to the VAT man every quarter. Unfortunately, these skills very often go against the core values of a great barista who, again like a chef, can tend to feel they're above that. Certain baristas can also tend to work and operate in a very laid back almost hippy like fashion. That can make for a very 'cool' environment to work in and visit but it can also produce a 'hey man, don't bother me with heavy stuff like the money', kind of attitude.

Unfortunately, the landlord will find that less appealing than your fellow staff or some of your customers.

A final flaw with a very barista driven shop can be that on occasion baristas are a little too 'cool for school'. This means that they can tend to value the coffee far more than basic politeness to the customer. It's actually quite common, so you'll need to be aware of this when recruiting baristas, even if you're not from this background yourself. The customer will see the barista like a head chef, i.e. they will want to interact with the barista far more than an ordinary member of staff or even the manager. It's the barista who, in a very coffee driven business, is the guy or girl who produces the magic. They see all sorts of banging and concentration going on and out pops a beautifully presented coffee at the end with perhaps a lovely little flourish of latte art. To the average punter that is magic so it's important that they get some acknowledgement and at least a smile from the barista when the coffee is being handed to them.

4. The money people

The money people are those, often extremely frustrating people, who look in on the industry and think 'hmmm, they must be making a bloody fortune in there. We need to get some of that.' We encounter a lot of this in our consulting business. People read our books or see us talk and think 'I'll get those guys in and they'll put something together for me. This time next year we'll be millionaires Rodney . . .'.

It very, very rarely works out like that because these folk so fundamentally lack the passion to produce something great. They simply won't grasp the fact that it actually takes a fair bit of money and passion to produce a great coffee shop. By its very nature a coffee shop needs to offer great coffee and hopefully something very tasty to eat. Great food and drink does not come off the back of a frozen food lorry or out of a cheap coffee machine with stale beans.

Furthermore, the money people will never grasp the fact that the design and ambience of a coffee shop is something that cannot just be thrown together with a small budget unless there is great care and (you guessed it) great passion.

The concept of the money people is best illustrated by a true story.

Café Culture

Mr Common Sense

We were once involved with a consultancy project to establish a chain of coffee bars within a number of retail sites. In essence, the project looked interesting. Many of the sites were decent and there seemed to be a decent initial will to do a good job.

The problem arose when what can only be described as too many cooks started to stir the broth. A variety of people were drafted in to do a variety of jobs and none of these people had even the slightest notion about how to run a coffee bar. This created a confusing design and an almost relentless meddling with the initial offer.

The real problem arose when an operations manager was appointed to 'pull the whole thing together'. This manager was the epitomy of 'Mr Common Sense'. There seemed to be little that he couldn't turn his hand to with a dismissive tone and a muttering of 'well, it's just common sense isn't it?'. He was also the type of chap who would turn to you with an earnest look in his eye and say profound things like 'the problem with common sense is that it isn't common . . .'. A pause would then be left for you to appreciate the pearl of wisdom (or indeed stifle a laugh – which was tricky because he'd be holding your gaze). To a large extent this is the equivalent of our ludicrous analogy that heart surgery is far easier than running a coffee shop since the heart only has about four tubes and a few flaps. Surely heart surgery is common sense? Perhaps not . . .

The real problem arose when, after we had specified a number of key suppliers who were highly experienced and had worked extensively with us in the past, Mr Common Sense decided to go out and negotiate. One of the key roles in running a business (as you'll discover in the people section) is to build a great team of suppliers round you who can support and help, even if times are tough (as they inevitably will be at times). It can takes years to build up these supplier relationships but they truly are like gold dust.

Mr Common Sense would arrive in and bully these suppliers to reduce their prices or, in many cases, to withdraw from the project. Ultimately, this meant that we ended up with a team who had been screwed to the ground with prices and existing suppliers who were increasingly resentful of being involved with the project. As you'll discover in the 'step by step' section these folk really need to be able to get on together. If a shop fitter doesn't talk to a catering supplier you end up with chaos and fridges that don't fit where they're supposed to go. And you also end up with a situation where nobody is taking responsibility, people are blaming each other and suppliers are trying to cut corners to get a little margin back into the project.

But worst of all is the fact that suppliers like bakers, coffee suppliers and sandwich makers really don't fully operate on common sense a lot of the time. It makes absolutely no sense for them to be fretting away about new recipes and working long into the night to produce little tweaks to already delicious products. Great food and drink (as you have grasped by now) is about passion. It has very little to do with common sense. If we applied common sense to our food we'd all just buy the cheapest food possible, boil it up and stick it in a blender. It would be fuel.

But that isn't what food is about, and it certainly isn't what it's about in a taste and inherently treat-driven environment like a coffee shop. The situation eventually collapsed in a pile of unpaid bills and disgruntled suppliers.

This experience still remains the most graphic example of how a coffee shop needs to be driven by passion first and money last for it to be successful that we've come across.

2   Taste

Passion coupled with pig headed determination will create taste that can stand up to the battering from the 'Scampi – they'll never know' guy at the back door (see story of Mervyn on page 60). It overcomes the desire to save money by using coffee that isn't quite fresh or serving a scone that's just a tiny bit burnt. Supplier relationships are key.

Out of the great passion that gets you started in the first place must come great products. Products that taste delicious and can 'hook and addict' the customer to keep coming back are at the cornerstone of any coffee shop. It's here that you need to dig really deep though. Many coffee shop owners think they can throw together a decent business with a second hand coffee machine and a couple of decent muffin recipes. Sadly those days, unless you have an exceptional location (and very low rent), are long gone.

> *Have the courage to say no. Have the courage to face the truth. Do the right thing because it is right. These are the magic keys to living your life with integrity.*
>
> W. Clement Stone

The growth of the speciality coffee shop, and in particular, the boundaries that Starbucks have smashed with pricing, have allowed an entirely new breed of coffee shop to grow and develop, and has also enabled people with much greater levels of expertise to make a decent living from owning a relatively simple coffee shop. This means that the competition out there is increasingly ferocious. And no matter how good a muffin or a brownie you think you can create in the Utopic confines of your kitchen, the consistent production of great food and coffee on a day-to-day basis is a totally different thing.

When we come back to the heart surgeon scenario, the one area that you need to be a specialist in is taste. Without great taste none of it will add up so this is where you have to go really, really deep. Between us we have hundreds of books on food and coffee. We endlessly debate over the most minute details in an effort to keep improving and keep exposing ourselves to new tastes and new ways to wow the customer. And we make really sure that above all we avoid the Mervyns of the world . . .

The great diluter of taste – Mervyn the Salesman

As you establish your business (and even before you open) you WILL, without a shadow of a doubt meet your version of 'Mervyn the Salesman'. Unsurprisingly this isn't his real name, though you may be lucky enough to find one who is actually called Mervyn. However, it's the principle that is at stake here and when you DO meet Mervyn, you need to strap on your best pig headed determination face.

Mervyn is a taste-robber. Mervyn actually doesn't really care about food. Mervyn cares about profit and convenience and systems and controls. Mervyn has a very low sense of what the customer actually thinks. In another life Mervyn is an oily politician or senior civil servant laughing at the pitiful masses as he pushes another bill through parliament wrapped up in red tape, secure in the knowledge that his cronies will benefit and the public is too stupid to be any the wiser.

The problem with Mervyn and this fairly unpleasant picture that has been created is that he is not quite as easy to identify as you might imagine. He has some pretty awesome tools in his armoury to help him change your way of thinking.

I first met Mervyn many, many years ago when we were running our sandwich bars. Mervyn, and all the other Mervyns in other similar companies, were the people who would tell us that it was simply impossible to source the kind of 'dry ham' (i.e. not injected full of water and formed out of ham 'stuff') that we wanted. Mervyn would insist that the turkey he supplied us with was the best in the world even though it looked a million miles away from what you might carve on a Christmas afternoon whilst nestling in the bosom of your squabbling family.

And then, every so often, Mervyn would arrive at the back door with a break through. Mervyn's break through wasn't that he had bothered his backside to actually source a little farmer who could supply him (and subsequently us) with a ham of exactly the quality that we needed. Oh no – that simply wouldn't compute for Mervyn. This is where Mervyn's politician-style contempt for the masses came in. Mervyn was always seeking easier and cheaper options. Mervyn is the sort of person who has driven chicken prices down to the level of a newspaper for a fully-prepared bird. So Mervyn's breakthough was always a cheaper version of what you already had and it was always accompanied with the immortal lines:

'The Customer Will Never Know'

The problem was that Mervyn had been in business for a long time and sometimes it was a little hard not to get taken in by his advice. If the implication is that you're stupid to be doing a different thing to what everyone else is doing (and according to Mervyn making great money out of it) just how easy it is to stick to your guns? Just how long will you hold out especially when you know that according to Mervyn, every sandwich you make using this new product will make you more money? What if Mervyn is actually correct and:

'The Customer Will Never Know'

The problem is that Mervyn is wrong and he continues to be a major part of everything that is wrong with the way that we buy and source our food. But Mervyn is simply too stupid to grasp this, and sadly the market for what they sell is actually quite large.

Things came to a head with our particular Mervyn one day when we were sourcing supplies for a new venture – a high class fish and chip business that was to cut no corners and to rewrite the rules in terms of quality within the local area. Mervyn still had the largest (government funded) frozen food storage facility out there and we still felt that it was worth giving him a try. Mervyn had also installed a new (government-funded) kitchen facility which allowed him to wow his customers with a vast array of cooked and uncooked mediocre products.

Specifically we were looking for a very high quality scampi to sell. Scampi is one of those great products (a little like a sausage) that can be made in a vast variety of ways. Shockingly bad quality scampi can also be made to look, to the Mervyns of this world, almost as good as the great stuff. So for Mervyn this was a dream sale.

Great scampi is made with big fresh prawns, sometimes even with their tails on, cooked in a light batter. It really is a delicious thing. One notch below that and you have smaller prawns and below that you have a sort of prawn sludge. At the very lowest level is a sort of fish gunk which is probably made up of all that fish poo at the bottom of the sea and then coloured to make it look a tiny little bit like a prawn colour. It's not nice.

So Mervyn reeled out his three products full of irritating sales statistics for all the people who currently use it. One of Mervyn's tricks is to tell you the name of a very busy (but rubbish) restaurant or bar that is using a certain product and then make a number of interesting eyebrow manoeuvres when you dismiss them for being rubbish. The inherent implication (which becomes stronger throughout a Mervyn meeting) is that you aren't fit to compare yourself to those people because they do such a huge volume of Mervyn's products.

We insisted that we didn't care about statistics or who currently used the products and that we were going to judge purely on taste and then look at the pricing. Then and only then would we consider how we might either fit the product to our price (possibly by altering portion size or increasing price) or look at other ways to get a product of that quality. This is where we had to dig into our bag and pull out our pig headed determination masks. It's also at this stage that Mervyn did something quite remarkable that has stuck in my memory in crystal clear detail.

My mask wasn't fully on so I wasn't arguing quite as strongly as my business partner, but his was firmly strapped on and he wasn't budging. Mervyn was insisting that the middle option of the three solutions (the sludge – not the fish poo product) he had presented was the correct product for us. He started to insist with great zeal that:

'The Customer Will Never Notice'

We continued to argue that we wanted to do something really special so we needed the better option. Mervyn insisted that his option was still a great product (possibly correct if you happened to be some type of bottom feeder) and that our preferred choice was really only for fancy restaurants.

My partner dug his heels and that's when Mervyn exploded into a rage. He ranted and raved about how we didn't know what we were talking about and how many years he had been working in the industry. His rage became so great that he had to be removed from the room by one of his (totally mortified) sales representatives.

We never used Mervyn again.

The chip shop was a huge success and went on to be voted the best fish and chop in Ireland. It became the first fast food outlet to be featured in the prestigious Bridgestone Irish Food Guide. It was immediately profitable and made substantial profits every year. We sold it, as a result of its great reputation, for a considerable sum more than a normal fish and chip shop might be sold.

Mervyn is everywhere and 99% of the time he is wrong. Taste is what matters and you simply cannot fool the customer for any long period of time. Please watch out for Mervyn and when he arrives or starts his arguments show him the door.

Henry Royce – the anti-Mervyn true story

Henry Royce (of Roll Royce fame) was wandering through his factory one day when he overheard two workers discussing a task they were working on. They were discussing whether the quality of what had been produced was up to standard. One worker insisted it was 'good enough' and they both carried on with what they were doing.

Royce went into a rage – 'Good enough' was NEVER good enough for a Rolls Royce he insisted. They could never be the type of company that produced cars that were 'good enough'. They needed to strive for perfection in everything that they did.

Royce was right about his cars, but exactly the same principle applies to your business. You simply cannot afford to put out food and drink that is 'good enough' – you need to strive for that perfect cup of coffee and perfect cookie or muffin every time.

The Mervyn the salesman story is crucial and absolutely fundamental to the development of your food and beverage offer. Your passion for some aspect of the business helps to drive you to create the products and to create your initial standards of taste. There will be something that sparked the idea off – a perfect cup of coffee, a perfect sandwich, a superb chocolate brownie or piece of cake. And it is out of this passion that your taste standards for all parts of your food and beverage offer need to evolve. But please understand that you *will* meet Mervyn and you will meet him in various forms. He can take the form of a lazy member of staff with a powerful personality who can persuade you to cut a corner. He can take the form of an outwardly successful business person who you may feel knows more than you. He can often take the form of an accountant. He will often take the form of a coffee supplier who has some super-duper machine that 'can do everything for you'.

The key thing is to relentlessly stick to the concept of **Integrity of Taste** that we use to govern our own businesses and is 100% inherent within our most successful clients. It's a fascinating experience to watch how emphatic a successful client is about not cutting corners.

Once you have established this **Integrity of Taste** as your base line you need to set up your rules for each product area and cast them in stone. These rules need to become etched in the brain of any suppliers or staff who are involved in product creation for you.

Our taste section splits off into two halves – closely linked obviously and both under the same 'Integrity of taste' umbrella, but very distinct as well. And if you really want to become brilliant at what you do and be a success you have no option but to go really deep in both areas

TASTE PART ONE – FOOD

Food, glorious food!
What is there more handsome?
Gulped, swallowed or chewed –
Still worth a king's ransom.
What is it we dream about?
What brings on a sigh?
Piled peaches and cream,
About six feet high!

Food, glorious food!
Eat right through the menu.
Just loosen your belt
Two inches and then you
Work up a new appetite.
In this interlude –
The food,
Once again, food
Fabulous food,
Glorious food.

From the musical *Oliver*

The food that you offer is an absolutely crucial part of your business. It's such an obvious statement but strangely one that is almost criminally overlooked by certain people within the industry. The reality is that if you simply rely on great coffee you will not survive unless you operate in very unusual and unique circumstances. The myth that there 'is a fortune to be made' in coffee shops is created by the simple fact that there is a very high percentage margin with coffee. Countless coffee shop customers (and potential owners) have sat round a table and calculated an arbitrary 20 or 30 pence of cost for the coffee and then looked in bewilderment at the price charged. The next thing you know they've remortgaged the house and are standing proudly signing contracts with a smirking estate agent and looking forward to the millions coming in.

But the problem is that a percentage margin is a very different thing from a pound note margin. And this is why you need food to accompany your coffee.

Johnny true story – Pound note versus percentage margin

The lack of understanding of the importance of actual pound note margins is something that has frustrated me endlessly over the years in a variety of different formats. The largest frustration comes from the fact that at the very pinnacle of the food and beverage industry (in terms of volume at least) many of the biggest contract caterers are still bound up by the concept that margins should be cast in stone. They take their managers through a tedious little training experience and shove them out the far side with a percentage margin goal tattoed onto the back of each hand and onto their foreheads so that it's the first thing they see as they bend over the sink in the morning wondering how their life has gone so badly wrong and why they are working in such a drone-like environment. Where did all those dreams of 'food glorious food' go wrong?

My first experience of this was when we were operating our sandwich bars many years ago. Our core product was a 'gourmet' sandwich which operated at the very top end of the market. As it sat on a shelf in a retail market it would generally represent no more than 33% of total sales. Obviously those figures varied from site to site but this was a reasonable rule of thumb. Because it was a unique product that nobody else was offering it was normally a fairly easy sell – particularly since we hadn't priced it at particularly aggressive level.

In those days the general rule of thumb (this has shifted in the last few years) was to offer the retailer 35% of the selling price for the sandwich. This was their profit. We only offered 30% though because we needed 70% to cover our costs. Ultimately it could be argued that our model was a trifle flawed and we should have passed this extra cost onto the customer, but as it stood, a canny independent retailer would quickly grasp that, even at 30%, he would make more money from our product than he would from a normal sandwich, i.e. more pounds and shillings in the till – NOT more percent on his profit and loss.

Here's how it worked:

Normal sandwich

Selling price – £1.50

Retailer profit margin at 35% – 52.5p

Our gourmet sandwich

Selling price – £2.00

Retailer profit margin at 30% – 60p

So for that little 5cm space on his shelf he was making an extra 7.5p from our products. If he sold 100 of our sandwiches a day that was a clear £7.50 of actual pound note profit that he could add to his bottom line, i.e. it made sound commercial sense to buy our product at a lower percentage margin than it did to buy the higher percentage margin cheaper product.

This may seem like a fairly simple sum, but it's absolutely crucial to grasp its importance and fully accept that you don't go to your bank with percentages. You don't pay your mortgage with a percentage and you'll certainly struggle to get away with giving your staff at the end of the week a generous envelope of percentages.

So the sum may seem simple and the concept should be clear, but that is rarely the case out in the marketplace. With our little bag of samples myself and my business partner trotted off to our local airport for a meeting with the head catering honcho. We presented our wares and they were very impressed. It seemed like we were going to easily make the sale. We then started to negotiate the price. We explained our discount structure and that's when it all paused. We were told that they simply couldn't operate at that level. I got out my piece of paper and explained that what we were offering was pound note profit and not percentage profit. I clearly articulated that they would make more money for every one of our sandwiches that they sold in comparison to the competition. None of this mattered though. They had strict guidelines that meant, no matter how much actual money they made, they had to achieve a gross margin target. They fully grasped that by not selling our product they would make less money but since the manager was rewarded for reaching gross margin percentage goals (and not pound note goals) there was absolutely no way we could do business. This shows one of the problems of incentivising purely in percentage terms (even though it is rife within the industry). Ultimately from this decision they would make less money, we would make less money, but the correct box in their financial reports was ticked.

The point of this story is not to illustrate how stupid they were (even though they were) or how there was a flaw in our model (there was and we ultimately changed it), but to show how the end goal is about pound notes in the till and how many of these you get to keep at the end of the week. It is not about percentage profit.

This, in a rather long-winded way, is where food comes in. Food has a lot of great uses within a coffee shop (which we'll come to) but at its most simple it allows you to increase average transaction size and the volume of pound note profit that you may have at the end of the day – even though the percentage margin will be considerably lower than the cup of coffee which is hopefully sold alongside it.

The holy grail of food though is to create products that are so great that they manage to drive people through the door at every stage of the day AND still allow you a great margin. There are, if you're clever both in your menu creation and marketing, various food products which can allow you gross margin percentages that might rival a cup of coffee.

How do you go about creating great food?

Well to reiterate a line that we're both very fond of saying, 'you go deep'. Very deep. With every main item group on your menu you need to become an expert. That means that you have to really understand each section at a level that allows you to competently create (either yourself or by instructing a chef or external supplier) something that is truly and quantifiably better than the competition. If you don't start with this as your goal then you're doomed to failure. Not because just producing something good, or even the same as the competition, is inherently wrong but because you will have your ideals diluted. Staff, equipment, suppliers, seasonality, delivery men, managers etc. will all conspire to dilute this lofty 'I must have the best ideal' by a few percent each. If you only aim to be good, you'll end up being mediocre. If you aim to be great, you stand a decent chance of being good and perhaps even very good.

To give you an example of these rules, we have included the sandwich rules that we would generally use to help a client create a new line of sandwiches. These rules are for a retail style pre-made sandwich that is aimed at a mid/upper middle market. A made to order sandwich rule list would be different, as would a list for a higher spec 'gourmet' offer. Some of the details are very specific and some are more general but all of them show just how deep and utterly pedantic you have to become in an effort to create an absolute world-class product that can and will help your business survive through any dips or troughs in the economy.

Sandwich rules – for mid-range retail sandwiches

- The protein part should be approximately 2 oz – a little over 50 g. This is the basis that all food costs need to come from.

- All sandwiches need to be costed to the pence.

- Presentation colour is essential for sandwich sales. For this reason it is very important to sometimes tweak ingredients and add a little colour (e.g. cress) without dramatically affecting taste.

- Salad should involve lettuce and tomato. Cucumber will quickly go soggy but can be used in certain situations. There should be three slices of tomato per sandwich.

- Lettuce should generally be mixed leaves or, for certain recipes, individual leaves such as rocket or watercress which specifically work for the filling. Darker lettuce such as rocket/endive/watercress will always look better in a pack than light lettuce such as iceberg.

- Fillings should be evenly distributed with a slight emphasis towards the centre section. It is essential that the cut sandwich looks generous and clearly has the described ingredients observable.

- Bacon should be crisp but not burnt. The UK palate will nearly always want back bacon but streaky can be experimented and tested.

- Mayonnaise should generally be full fat unless the sandwich is a specifically healthy offer. Taste should take precedence over 'healthiness' in 90% of situations but always have healthy alternatives.

- Spreads help to 'waterproof' the bread but increase fat and do little for taste. They need to be experimented with but are generally not used.

- Pork sandwiches have a short shelf life and simply don't sell.

- Ham needs to be of high quality with as little fat as possible.

- Any seasoning should generally be put on the protein part of the sandwich and not on the salad. Seasoning can also be incorporated into mayonnaise.

- White pepper is a better alternative than black pepper for a pre-packed sandwich since black pepper can be perceived as grit or dirt.

- Bread quality is paramount. Tastes will vary (between brown/white/wholemeal etc.) but freshness is essential. Experiment and test between different bread types.

- Some non-mayonnaise selections are essential.

- Mayonnaise can easily be flavoured to help put a subtle twist to sandwiches.

- Think about colour, presentation and texture as well as taste.

- The market expects free range eggs but not free range chicken yet. Free range chicken is almost prohibitively expensive to put in a sandwich but this will hopefully change soon.

- Sales will generally be split (although this must be tested from site to site) about two thirds classics and one third specials. Specials can be charged at up to 50% more than the classics and allow an excellent lift in pound note margin.

- It is worth creating a set number of excellent sandwiches to begin with and then building on that. Keep the number relatively low and ensure they are perfect before moving on.

- Roasted tomatoes produce a very intense burst of flavour and can work well with a variety of classics (e.g. egg). If there is no facility to roast then sunblush or sundried can provide a great burst of taste.

- Onion greatly improves the taste but will generally put more people off than it attracts in a pre-prepared sandwich (again it should be tested). Grated onion (or onion salt) can dramatically improve a savoury flavour in meat sandwiches without the hardshness.

■ Avocado needs lemon juice to avoid it going brown. It works well with crayfish, bacon, brie and chicken (not all together) but is a brave choice and not advisable initially.

■ Old classics such as Coronation chicken have recently become popular again. Generally raisins will be picked out though and should be avoided.

■ Beef sandwiches (whilst undoubtedly delicious) don't sell in great quantities and the price of beef is often prohibitive (unless buying very poor quality).

■ Lamb is very difficult to sell.

■ Smoked bacon has extra flavour and is only slightly more expensive.

■ Chicken will always sell very well. Regardless of what we may feel in terms of taste, ultimately the UK palate wants chicken breast and that must be catered for.

Key mantras

The important thing to grasp from that rules list is that it must apply to every product that you have. Then you can refine it down into a few key mantras. One of the mantras that should evolve for all your food should be 'we don't cut corners'. These mantras need to be the things that most clearly help to articulate the passion and initial vision that you had with your original idea.

The mantras also help to make sure that you don't get your concept diluted. The dilution of a concept is something we see and experience every day in life. It generally takes very small dilutions in just a few areas to end up with a concept that bears no resemblance to the original idea. But if you can develop a couple of clear mantras that you stick to (even when you know it is irritating people) then your concept becomes much harder to dilute. After a while you start to catch members of staff repeating these mantras and saying to co-workers 'we don't cut corners', or whatever it is, and it starts to seep into the very core of your business. When this happens you can have a much greater sense of peace when you're lying on the beach secure in the knowledge that someone has got up at 5.00 a.m. to bake your scones and won't be 'cutting corners' because a Mervyn character arrived at the back door with a scone mix promising 'The Customer Will Never Know'.

Star products

Once you have established your basic rules and developed a mantra for each of your main products, then you then need to move onto the creation of your star products. It is your star products that will really help to differentiate you from everyone else and these are the things that will hopefully form the myth and the legend around your business that sets the 'word of mouth' tongues wagging.

Star or 'hero' products can really be anything but they must be something that is truly delicious and has evolved over time to help create a great story. These are the sorts of products that visiting local celebrities (or past Big Brother contestants) need to be snapped eating so that you can help grow the myth and legend that surrounds them. Ideally they need to be easily portable for takeway too and shouldn't, if at all humanly possible, be too obviously loaded with calories. You want your customer to feel they can have one every day of the week rather than just a treat on Friday.

Examples of star products include:

- A muffin made from a unique recipe that has been passed down through the family.

- A cinnamon roll.

- Apple and cinnamon cakes.

- A scone made with a recipe that incorporates a classic local ingredient.

- A chocolate brownie that truly stands out from the crowd.

- A large cookie that has a little twist in the recipe.

- A flapjack that has a few different or luxury ingredients.

- A twist on a local speciality that makes it the best available.

- A carrot cake/banana cake etc. that is freshly made daily and served in a unique manner, perhaps with walnuts or a certain spice.

- A twist on (or just an exceptionally good version of) classic traybakes such as millionaire's shortbread, malteser buns, fifteens, florentines, shortbread etc.

- A triple decker sandwich.

- The perfect bacon sandwich in the morning with a variety of bread choices.

▪ An age old coffee cake recipe handed down from your grandmother.

▪ A recipe for a lunch item that you prised from a little coffee shop owner in Rome/New York/Paris etc.

▪ A twist on a local recipe for a bun.

▪ A larger version of a local bun.

▪ A fresher recipe of a local bun.

▪ A recipe for a local bun that uses better ingredients.

▪ A better packaged version of a local bun.

▪ A savoury version of a classically sweet recipe.

The list is far from exhaustive but the key factor is that it's something that has YOUR story behind it. It ideally needs to be *your* recipe or one that has been passed down through a couple of generations in your family. *You* want control over it – not the baker or employee who dreamt it up. Or perhaps it was something that you saw on holiday and had to beg the owner of the establishment to give you the recipe. It's likely that this product probably was an integral part of your original vision and the passion that helped (or will help) to drive you to open. It mustn't be fake either. The story has to be true (although it can be slightly romanticised) because if it's false you'll not be able to properly convey it with passion. It must reek of genuine pride. The large chains rely on fake marketing led stories all the time and customers are tired and jaded with them.

This product then needs to become a cornerstone of your marketing and must have a prominent position within the store. You obviously don't want to ram it down your customer's throats but it should, very obviously, be something that they should want to try.

A word of caution though. Never forget this whole enterprise is about making money. Your star product must reflect this. Select a star product with a low margin at your peril. The last thing you want to be doing, once you have created a sales success, is realise it dosen't produce a lot of profit.

What should you sell?

Your general food offer needs to reflect the original vision and passion but it must also be commercial. There is a difficult and confusing line to be walked between passion, vision and commercial success, but the essence is that you need to have great products for sale throughout the day without being all things to all people. The temptation to start offering items that fall outside of the initial vision simply because of a customer suggestion or because your sales are slow, is one that needs to be resisted. Any new product development must fit within the vision and the ability that you have with existing facilities to create a new product to the necessary standard.

The coffee shop model

Let's take an arbitrary coffee house model that exists in a relatively busy location where there are potential sales available throughout the day from about 7.30 a.m. to 5.00 p.m. Different models will have different opening hours and be aware that these can change. There has been a recent trend and increasing acceptance of the coffee house as somewhere to go in the evening instead of the pub, so operators who tried (unsuccessfully) opening in the evening five years ago should test again now to see if there has been enough of a change to warrant a re-think.

In our fictional coffee house model we'll break the day down and look at a few key products which might work for each section.

7.30 a.m. to 9.00 a.m.

During this zone we are generally dealing with people in a rush. They want a coffee hit and ideally they will be so addicted to your product that they have been thinking about it for the previous half hour as they journey in to work. But the essence here is speed so we want to sell them something to eat at the same time that doesn't take a lot of time to serve, or also annoy customers behind who are also in a rush.

The offer could reflect classic French breakfast items (albeit in an Anglicised way) like croissant, pain au raisin or pain au chocolat. All of these can be bought in a part baked format and the quality is often very good. Alternatively you can have a variety of filled sandwich/rolls with breakfast style ingredients (egg, bacon, sausage etc.). For the healthy folk you need smoothies, fresh fruit salads and fruit compote/yoghurt and granola mixes. All of these items can be picked up easily and require absolutely no preparation.

One notch above this are various baked pastries and scones which need a quick zap in the microwave and are then served with butter. There are a variety of fruit/cinnamon scones that can work very well in this way and shouldn't slow your queue down.

A final notch up in terms of speed and hassle (bear in mind this unit has no extraction) is to offer breakfast style panini/toasted sandwiches or ciabatta. If you are going to do this it is vital that you remove the production process from the normal till and barista line. You will shoot yourself in the foot commercially if this slows the queue by trying to just slot it into your standard operation. Speed will always remain the most important thing at this time of day – forget that at your peril.

With a kitchen and adequate extraction facilities you can look at much more sophisticated breakfast offers and it is worth bearing in mind that this is an increasingly growing market.

9.00 a.m. to 11.30 a.m.

During this zone you really need to be making good money. Again, this will vary from site to site but this is where you can mix the holy grail (in margin terms) of a great bun offer and coffee. Depending on what your market is you will need to tweak the offer a little but you must have at least one star or hero product in this zone that is so good that your customers can't stop thinking about it whilst sitting at their desk or if they're out doing a bit of shopping.

This section of the day is where you will hope to make really good money. Your spend should be reasonable and the bun and coffee marriage is a match made in margin heaven. So you really need to focus on creating an offer that makes it seem unusual for your customers to be drinking a cup of coffee on its own.

You need to make sure that your offer, and the star product in particular, at this stage fills a number of criteria.

- It must be delicious but not too calorie laden. At the very least your customers must be able to kid themselves that it's not too fattening. If you have something that is too obviously fattening, then no matter how delicious it is you'll really struggle to sell it any day other than Friday.

- It really must be unique. It needs to be measurably better than that which is produced by your competition. We have to assume that your site isn't going to be quite as good as the big chains, so you're expecting your customers to go slightly out of their way to get to you. They'll only do that for something really delicious.

■ It must have a high margin. Forget about producing something with extravagantly expensive ingredients. Keep it relatively simple and price it bravely so that it sells but has a high perceived value.

■ Create a great story around it. It cannot have been just thrown together in a weekend.

■ Ideally this product should be a freshly baked product on a daily basis. This helps to increase your perceived difference to the chains.

Some examples of the types of product that you can be selling successfully during this part of the day are scones, pastry rolls, muffins and tea cakes. Essentially, we are talking about bread products with a little twist.

On a consistent basis it is essential to measure average spend during this time of day and ensure that you are selling as many 'bun and coffee' combos as possible. At its most simple you can just count coffees sold during this time period and compare this with numbers of buns sold. You need to be working on improving this ratio at all times.

11.30 a.m. to 2.30 p.m.

Lunch time trade will vary enormously depending on your model but again you need to be balancing what people want and expect with a few tweaks and surprises to 'hook and addict' them.

Everything you produce here should be mindful of the types of customer you have. How long will they have for lunch? What sort of budget will they have? Will they be alone just grabbing 'fuel' or are they likely to be eating with friends or colleagues? Are they health conscious? Will they need an ability to take food away to eat at their desk?

Questions like these need to be at the forefront of your menu creation. It's back to that old 'message to market match' that we discussed in the positioning section. You can produce the best food in the world but if it doesn't fit the purchasing criteria of the customer then you're sunk.

Whatever you do decide to do though, it has to be delicious. Cater almost exclusively towards normal eaters and ensure that taste is your number one criteria. Vegetarians and people with allergies are in a much smaller minority than they like to think they are and you must be careful about exposing yourself to too great a choice for these (sometimes incredibly vocal) minorities at the expense of normal paying customers. It's easy to find yourself bullied by some of these groups to provide a wide choice for them. You'll quickly realise that they won't sell and you'll have missed out on rule number one – it's a commercial venture! You're here to make money.

Your lunchtime offer will have a slightly lower margin than the morning offer but the spend will be higher so you're well ahead of the game. Again this is a section where you need to be maximising revenue as much as possible so it's vital that you watch your key ratios and try to improve on them at all times.

Through your merchandising and subtle selling at the till (subtle being the important part of that sentence), you ideally want every customer to buy a savoury dish, a cold drink, a sweet dish and a cup of coffee. Obviously they won't, and in reality only a tiny fraction will, but that's your goal. That's what you need to keep in mind as you craft a menu and design your flows.

Ninety percent of your customers will be tight for time at lunch so it's vital that you manage to make the process relatively painless for them to buy and eat quickly. It's all a delicate balance and you'll see in the people section a few techniques to help you view things from their perspective and ultimately increase your sales.

2.30 p.m. to 5.00 p.m.

This is the dead zone for many coffee shops and if you can find a site that will be busy during these hours it will make a huge difference to your profitability. Sites that are near primary schools can do well here since they will have mothers grabbing a quick coffee as they pick up their kids or taking the kids out for a treat after school. Make sure your menu reflects this with kids-based items like mini cookies, ice creams, brightly coloured biscuits, mini muffins and a variety of kids drinks including some healthy ones.

Being beside a school for older children is a mixed blessing. You can be fairly certain of extra customers but the spend will be low and teenagers can be quite remarkably annoying to other customers. It's one that you'll have to judge for yourself and if you want to encourage or discourage them you may have to alter your menu (and pricing) accordingly.

The general afternoon offer will be very similar to what you have in the morning. The only issue you have is that you'll need to be careful to keep the balance between 'abundant' looking bakery products (which always sell better than the last one or two in a dish) and having too much wastage.

Cake should be a vital part of your afternoon sales mix. It's a relatively tough sell in a somewhat health obsessed environment, but a superb coffee cake or chocolate cake will always be a magnificent partner for coffee.

Keep innovating

Google thrives on launching products quickly and then letting users tell us what needs improving. We really focus on failing wisely, there is no penalty for failure. In fact we encourage it because if you're not failing it means you're probably not trying.

Matt Glotzbach, product management director

It's very easy to become complacent about your menu so you must have a formal process of innovation put in place. Your customers will become bored with what you offer and the big chains are very good at constantly producing 'new!' items on their menu at every stage of the day. Your model needs to have its own rules but you should ensure that regardless of what you sell, you have consistent change every few weeks or so. Remove stars and old faithfuls from your menu at your own risk though. You need to have a basic core of products that sell well and keep the regulars returning every day. Only innovate and produce new products in addition to those items.

Johnny true story

Back in the early days of my career in our first sandwich bar I felt that I didn't need to innovate. I felt that our product was so great that we really didn't need to bother improving it. The reality was, at this stage, that was almost true. We had very little competition and some very good basic products. I felt that my energies were far better used in developing the business and opening new sites – i.e. expanding my ego rather than making sure we were making the maximum profit from the existing sites.

One loyal and regular customer called Ernie (in this case actually his real name!) quietly took me to one side and suggested that I put a few extra things on the menu. He said that coming in every day he was starting to get a little bored with what we had. He emphasised just how much he still loved our product and explained that for him our sandwich bar was a little oasis of excitement away from the tedium of running his printing business. But he would just like to see something new on the board every now and then.

Like the youthful know-it-all idiot that I was, I basically argued with him. I told him that we had loads on the menu and why didn't he just try a few new things. A few months later he asked me again. I promised I'd look into it and again pretty much dismissed him. We were very busy as it was – why would I bother complicating things?

Finally, I started to notice that he simply wasn't coming in so much. We were still busy but also a heck of a long way off full capacity and slowly and painfully the penny dropped. We'd lost a chunk of business through a combination of laziness and an arrogance that our customers would just keep coming back if we provided the same great stuff every day.

Don't make the same mistake in your business. People look to you for change and excitement. They get plenty of the same old stuff day in and day out in their jobs.

Throughout the day don't ever forget that your coffee is your best hook. There is lots going on in each of these daily niches with food, speed, service and innovation but consistently well prepared coffee will be the key to building that profitability. If you give somebody a poor experience because you are focusing on speed in the morning or forget about freshness rules in the afternoon they simply will not come back. It is a fine line.

TASTE PART TWO – COFFEE

> *One more cup of coffee for the road,*
> *One more cup of coffee 'fore I go,*
> *To the valley below.*
>
> Bob Dylan

Running coffee shops and associated businesses is hard work and there are many factors that all need to be aligned. However, if there is one single piece of advice that you should take from us, the one big thing, by far the most important factor, and the one that will make the most difference on its own, it's **your coffee offer**.

We have built very successful businesses on a good coffee offer, and Hugh has spent most of his life living this, as have many other people – because if you get it right, it can transform everything about your business. Here are a few excellent reasons for following this advice.

Quality

Everything about great taste drives people to buy coffee. The key principle is to hook and addict your customer to great tasting drinks. You need to understand what tastes good and what is not acceptable (and many experienced operators do not know this). You have to have a very clear understanding of what your end game is and that means careful analysis of every detail of your coffee offer. If you focus on cleanliness, freshness and extraction, you will be 80% there. Lookout for this module in The Coffeeboys Coffee Production programme or email: coffee 80% to moreinfo@freecoffeeboys.com. And don't forget tea. Much more on how to identify all this later.

Actual product quality of everything else

When you make a special effort with your coffee you will have to allocate reasonable resources to the project. This then raises your expectation – of everything else! You will want to make sure that the other poor products are, to quote one of Johnny's favourite sayings, 'brought up a notch'. Your coffee can inspire more than your customers.

Customer loyalty

Believe it or not great coffee is consistently hard to find and if you provide it people will go out of their way, not only to get your coffee, but rave about how good it is to others. Don't be foolish enough to let that new customer who is already sold on your quality receive a disappointing experience. Remember the old rant that happy customers tell an average of three people and unhappy ones tell ten. Remember the old adage that customer satisfaction is worthless but customer loyalty is priceless. Satisfied customers will buy their coffee anywhere. Loyal customers will encourage others to buy from you and **fight** before they switch, so don't ever forget if a customer is fighting with you there is a golden opportunity to secure their business for another long period by doing whatever you have to do to resolve their problem. It is *always* worth it.

Marketing

With a great product in place you can now tell everybody how good it is. That's basic marketing and, done well with good planned outcomes and measurement in place, it can really make a difference to your business.

Staff satisfaction and motivation

Like your product, your staff (who are a vital part of your product) will be much happier producing and selling a better quality coffee. If you build into the plan a barista training programme, and perhaps even encourage them to enter a competition, then they will quickly feel that they have real expertise and this is massively motivational. The World Barista Championships start with regional heats in every country and the SCAE UK Chapter run a brilliant competition every year that is easy to enter and not at all intimidating. Its also great fun and your staff will get an enormous amount from networking with other baristas and exchanging opinions and ideas. This **will** have a direct and positive impact on your business.

Customer service

With awareness of what great coffee should taste like and staff that genuinely care, it makes obvious sense that overall customer service will improve because they will know more, be more confident and, importantly, their peers will have raised the bar as well so there will be less room for complacency. This should be a constant management message. Great customer service means making each experience memorable. You can do that with coffee. And don't be fooled by the startling number of businesses who boast 97.5% customer satisfaction – just look at their coffee. Hello! Welcome to FantasyLand.

Profits

The bottom line is that it will improve your bottom line. Getting customers to come back for more and tell potential new customers is the holy grail of marketers and there is no better product to implement this kind of activity with than coffee.

We have added value to hundreds of coffee offers in a wide range of sectors and the one thing that absolutely always amazes us is just how effective (and for us easy) properly fixing the coffee offer is. It does mean making sure that you avoid Mervyn the salesman, who is out there in many guises preaching and selling his wares to the unsuspecting coffee buyer who may not even be a coffee drinker and is generally too busy doing what he does (and probably like the rest of us under pressure) to figure out what the key to good coffee is.

You will probably have heard from many people that the coffee bar business is all about location, location, location and they are not entirely wrong. What we know, however, is that while it may be the single most important business factor it only becomes so if the offer is right. If you have a mediocre or even a poor offer and a captive audience then you will still sell volume – just not anywhere near your potential. The managers of these businesses, particularly if they are chains, usually lack the entrepreneurial touch that you always get with an owner operator. They are generally more interested in systems that put speed and convenience before taste. Most of these guys don't even know that they don't know how important taste is.

This is such an important factor for you to grasp that we have three stories to illustrate the point. Crucially the same rules apply to secondary locations and actually become even more important.

Hugo true story – Quality Coffee Act I

We talked to an institutional site for years that used a coffee product that was fast, portion controlled with no waste, keenly priced and was no hassle. It worked and there were no complaints. Our view was that we could significantly increase sales by selling a great tasting coffee product but this meant training all the staff, more cleaning, more hassle and more cost. We also knew from experience that a trial would probably not work because all the standard objections would come out, we would be subjected to the 'it'll never work' brigade and relegated quickly to the 'it didn't work' pile.

With no option to get in without a trial however, we succumbed and invested heavily in the right solution even though it was a risk. It worked gloriously. We trebled sales in the first year and have maintained single digit growth every subsequent year by implementing a good marketing calendar strategy and working hard at it.

That was in 1995.

Hugo true story – Quality Coffee Act II

We talked to another captive audience site again for a long time trying to convince them that what they did just wasn't good and that if they improved it they would reap significant reward. They had a major supplier and leading brand name in place and their area sales manager and representatives regularly called in to talk about the weather and local news, perhaps dealing with a few minor complaints that involved a couple of free cases of products or another training session from their award winning training school.

Eventually we got our nose in, changed the coffee offer, and by the end of the first year sales had doubled from 500 to 1,000 cups per day. This was easily another £100,000 on their bottom line after all the expenses such as extra equipment costs and staff training were accounted for.

That was in 2001.

Hugo true story – Quality Coffee Act III

This time we looked at a vacant site in a key area that had massive potential as a coffee bar. The problem was that it was only three-square meters. We created a turnkey coffee bar brand from scratch focusing on a great coffee offer that was fantastic value. We also added, in true Coffeeboys style, a great bun offer to match the coffee.

Regular customers rave about the great quality cappuccinos and lattes and the delicious Ethiopian filter coffee that is fruity and smooth. Many say they can't get through the day without one of our coffees. This is the power of great coffee. This is the power of great taste. Thousands of specialty coffees are sold each week on this site contributing significantly to the bottom line of this organisation.

That was in 2006.

Notice that the importance of getting your coffee right is timeless, requiring some adjustment to take account of trends and new technology, but fundamentally it is based on getting great taste in the cup. Generally, people who sell coffee under deliver on this and in some cases dramatically more than, in our opinion, you can get away with. When this happens with the large chains, and it does, it presents a brilliant opportunity for those who can execute and take advantage of the slow corporate decision-making process by acting with speed, care and attention, and above all, awareness that it's all about the coffee.

So, in the immortal words of Bob Dylan, it's just one more cup of coffee to get you to the valley below. That valley is full of cash.

Methods of brewing

One of our favourite rants is the brewing method wine metaphor. It sort of says it all in one sense and yet demonstrates the need to dig deeper into this very basic decision.

Instant is your sweet/cheap wine.

Filter is your House – its good or bad depending where you go.

Espresso is your trendy Sauvignon or Rioja.

And then you go full circle to Single Estate's that are your Bordeaux & Burgundy.

In your business many salesmen will tell you that the Espresso method of brewing is the only one to consider and it is indeed the price of entry. Milk-based drinks are essential to your coffee business and latte is king. You cannot seriously operate a coffee business without espresso equipment and it is also one of the biggest investments you will make – so the coffee mis-salesman is just like our Mervyn and will tell you that you need to use it for regular coffee as well so that he can justify his price. Beware.

Of course Coffee Mervyn will also tell you that it's fresh and there is no waste and he might even try to persuade you to use a fully automatic bean to cup machine because it means less staff training and better consistency. He needs a b*llsh*tometer on almost a daily basis.

Lets just say that you need to ensure you are talking to a good salesman who not only knows the product but has the desire to put your needs and interest first and persuade you to buy the right thing. The problem is that there are many 'experts' out there that genuinely *think* they know how to do this. So I have two sets of questions that you should ask the salesman. Luckily you will be able to dismiss Coffee Mervyn very quickly, but your objective should be to smoke out his colleagues who are a bit smarter and equally capable of scoring highly with the meter.

Q1. Where have you sold this model to recently?

Q2. Would they be happy for me to call?

Q3. Who else would refer you?

If they satisfactorily answer these questions without stuttering then ask:

Q1. Will you give me my money back if I change my mind?

Q2. Will you rent or loan the equipment out?

Q3. Is it ok if I don't sign a contract?

and with three Yes's then proceed carefully to Go!

Focus on filter coffee

What we have sold for years is the ability to control the brewing factors that create that personal coffee moment for YOUR customers and those brewing factors are so widely misunderstood that it provides such a brilliant opportunity.

In today's turbulent world everybody talks about their quality coffee and they use tools like Fairtrade or organic or whatever their equipment salesman has taught them.

Everyone is an expert, and many are armed and dangerous with parts of stories and partial facts that they vocalise without anybody challenging them on what they are saying. Everyone has their own story to tell. This is a very good thing because we need to understand that the story is the key to a good marketing and sales plan, but that story needs to stand up to rigor and scrutiny.

You can no longer simply claim that you are environmentally and socially delivering with your sustainable product unless you can back it up.

So how do you do this in an easy, inexpensive, reasonably straightforward, highly effective and above all a real quality way (the only road to increasing bottom line)?

Get into single-origin filter brewed coffee as your regular brew and teach everybody how to buy it!

Here are three great reasons why:

1. Great coffee is about freshness, cleanliness and extraction. If you know The Coffeeboys' material you will know that by now. If you are new to The Coffeeboys this is one of our mantras. And extraction is the key. Extraction = Taste and Taste = Profit. Filter coffee is brewed in five minutes and allows you to create reasonably easily a fabulous flavor profile – fruit, acidity, chocolate, sweetness and body jumping all over those taste buds.

    Have you ever tasted a wonderful Ethiopian Yirgacheffe, an amazing Colombian Huila or a magnificent El Salvador Finca La Fany? You simply have to get into educating your customers on amazing coffees like these. If you don't have an amazing filter from a great region, isn't it time that you wised up and smelt the real coffee . . . and profit?

    It is not by accident that we keep ranting about the money because you need to understand, again and again, that while sourcing amazing coffee, taking great care in brewing it and 'controlling the brewing factors' and then marketing it to your loyal customers is a big effort (and will cost you more). You need to realise that in these times where the consumer's pound or euro is going to be hard fought over – that the only way to get that spend is to be better than anybody else. Those that make the effort, take action, and consistently apply factors and principles to their business, will win.

    Those businesses that do the right thing will always prevail over those that don't.

2. Speed is one of the key factors in driving the bottom line for a busy coffee bar. Clearly a good location ensures that you have enough people who want to buy coffee, but we see so many high street businesses who have great locations, good marketing and branding, high quality fixtures and fittings, have made at least an attempt to train staff and create a good working environment and then get it so wrong by only offering espresso-based beverages. These take longer to make, are labour intensive, are much more difficult to control regarding consistency (which is the holy grail of any cuisine business), and irritate the most important person to your business – your customer. Today's customer has no time and very little

patience. We are in the era of the never satisfied customer and they don't want to be told that good coffee takes more of the one thing they are short of – time.

In addition, brewing a great filter coffee takes the pressure off the espresso machine extending its life, reducing service costs and eliminating the need for several expert baristas to be on duty each shift.

3. We are in the twilight of a society based on data. As information and intelligence become the domain of computers, everybody is placing more value on the one human factor that cannot be automated: emotion. The language of emotion will affect everything from our coffee purchasing decisions to how we work with others. Businesses will thrive on the basis of their stories and myths and we need to understand that the products are less important than the stories but of course that is only if the products are very very good. This, in our view, is today's price of entry.

Choosing and marketing a fantastic filter coffee for your business has the ability to tick many of the boxes required to tell a good story.

■ It can be fully traceable right back to the farm meaning that it simply cannot be more authentically and ethically sourced. This knocks many other stories about fairness and origin for six.

■ You can tell the customer the price you paid for it in terms of percentage. New York 'C' is around $1.15/lb and Fairtrade is $1.42 at the time of writing, so asking your supplier the green price for this purpose allows you to say that you have paid 25% more than the Fairtrade price and this will only cost you pence. This is also easily recoverable in your selling price. Why don't you buy the best coffee you possibly can and charge an extra 10p more than offsetting any additional cost? And don't forget – if your coffee supplier doesn't tell you or doesn't know the answers . . . its time to look for a professional.

■ It can deliver on the taste profile that you describe in a way that espresso can never match. Additionally, every cup can taste the same giving you the ability to compare, discover and educate your customer. We have spent years teaching people how to buy rather than selling them coffee.

■ It can cost less to produce and with the ability to brew specific taste profiles allows you to charge a premium for what you are describing –

only of course if you take enough care to prepare it properly. It has to be worth what ends up in the cup and it is your responsibility to get perfect.

Espresso-based coffee

Espresso is a method of brewing that was invented in Italy by Luigi Bazzera. It means 'quick' and involves controlling a number of brewing factors to produce a small approximate 35ml shot that is then consumed on its own, brewed shorter as a ristretto or longer as a lungo. It is also most commonly used in this country as a base for a range of espresso beverages with milk, namely cappuccino and latte. So the bottom line is that you have to immerse yourself in the coffee world and get a good grasp of the brewing factors like grinding, dosing, packing, extraction rates and volume recipes. You cannot effectively sell espresso-based coffee if you don't fully understand the cuisine.

Our advice is to teach yourself through joining organisations like The Speciality Coffee Association of Europe or America, entering your local Barista Championship which leads to The World Barista Championships, or find yourself one of many passionate and really excellent coffee suppliers who specialise in training customers who buy their coffee or equipment.

There is also a very lively barista internet culture. They are a great bunch of people who have a fantastic attitude to helping others in the industry by sharing information and knowledge. Barista Jams are particularly useful events to attend, as are the many exhibitions and coffee-related conferences that are run and attended every year by the industry experts and operators. Take responsibility for learning and start with the internet.

The truth about coffee labels

Fairtrade

Fairtrade coffee is coffee that has been purchased from farmers (usually peasant farmers) at a 'fair' price as defined by the brand Fairtrade. The extra paid to these farmers under Fairtrade arrangements is extremely modest. There are many sustainable coffee offers that make a much more substantial contribution to farmers using the relationship model where coffee is selected primarily on taste rather than certification and is much more ethical. However we must be fair to Fairtrade, if you excuse the pun, for raising awareness and also give them credit for a brilliant name in marketing terms.

Organic

Organic coffee is coffee that has been certified by a third-party agency as having been grown and processed without the use of pesticides, herbicides, or similar chemicals.

Unfortunately, it is totally impractical and unfeasible in our opinion for some of the most amazing coffee regions in the world to produce coffee without using chemicals.

UTZ Kapeh

This means 'a good cup of coffee'. Its vision is to achieve sustainable agricultural supply chains where farmers are professionals, implementing good practices which lead to better businesses. It contains criteria on soil, fertilizer, waste pollution, worker health, safety and welfare and other socio economic and cultural conduct.

It is probably the most feasible certification model where the producer is rewarded in a market orientated way and not in the form of a minimum price. Therefore UTZ Kapeh does not interfere in the price negotiations between parties who buy on taste.

Shade

This describes coffee grown under a shade canopy. It is traditionally grown in shade in many (but not all) parts of Mexico, Central America, Colombia, Peru, and Venezuela, and in some other parts of the world, including India and some regions of Indonesia and Africa. Elsewhere coffee is traditionally grown in full sun, or near full sun. The importance of maintaining shade canopies to supply habitat for migrating song birds in Central America has led to a controversial campaign by researchers at the Smithsonian Institute and their supporters to define 'shade grown' in rather narrow terms (shade provided by mixed native trees) and label coffees grown under such a native canopy as 'bird friendly'. Another good story perhaps, but in our view has no direct effect on the taste.

Rainforest Alliance

The Rainforest Alliance works to conserve biodiversity and ensure sustainable livelihoods by transforming land-use practices, business practices and consumer behavior. This is another story that is developed by marketing departments to fit with sustainable values that are communicated at every opportunity to the consumer.

Decaffeinated

Speciality coffees are decaffeinated in the green state, currently by one of four methods. The direct solvent method involves treating the beans with solvent, which selectively removes the caffeine from the beans by steaming. The indirect solvent, or solvent-water method, involves soaking the green beans in hot water, removing the caffeine from the hot water by means of a solvent, and recombining the water with the beans, which are then dried. Both processes using solvents often are called European Process or Traditional Process. The water-only method, commonly known by the proprietary name Swiss Water Process TM, involves the same steps, but removes the caffeine from the water by allowing it to percolate through a bed of activated charcoal. In the carbon dioxide method, which is only beginning to be established in the specialty-coffee trade, the caffeine is stripped directly from the beans by a highly compressed semi-liquid form of carbon dioxide. That's the technical bit. To us decaffeinated has traditionally lacked flavour, but I must admit to tasting some great decaffeinated products recently, so we are going to change our long held view here and say it is possible to get some great decaffeinated coffee's but – keep judging it in taste.

Flavoured

These are coffees that in their roasted, whole-bean form have been mixed with flavouring agents. A complete waste of time in business terms as far as we are concerned, and as for taste – well lets just say no more.

Equipment reality

This is a big area, often misunderstood, and regularly the subject of controversy, claims and counter claims from the hundreds of manufacturers out there all scrapping for market share.

We believe that there is no such thing as a rubbish product that has stood the test of time because, quite simply, the consumer is much smarter than that. Today's customer has much more savvy and can tell when they are being mis-sold most of the time. So lest we get ourselves in trouble with the many equipment people that we know and love – let us make a few observations that, if you take heed of, we feel sure you won't be going too far wrong.

Consider the sales person, not the model. The key to great equipment is the person who will take responsibility for the service and maintenance. Have they been in the business long ? How many service engineers do they employ? What is their response time? Who are their customers? Then take the trouble to verify the claims by asking for referrals – this will always separate the men from the boys!

Never ever buy the entry-level model in any range. Manufacturers, like everybody else need to make a profit, and they all have entry level models that have all sorts of corners cut. The top of the range may well present the opposite problem so make sure you ask all the relevant questions and then go one better than you think. The best selling model is often a good place to start, but don't forget customers can get it very wrong sometimes, and in staggeringly big numbers. Just ask any Italian who loves his coffee what not to buy and nine times out of ten he will tell you the same brand – which never ceases to amaze me.

Be really careful with bean to cup equipment. They require a high degree of technical competence to manage and maintain. They also require more service. However, with the right solution there is little doubt that they can be an excellent tool in the pursuit of consistency, and properly selected and set up can be better than many traditional operations. The key is your partner. Please make sure you don't deal with Equipment Mervyn in this critical coffee business decision.

Hugo true story – Taste

For years I have ranted on about how important it is in my business to ask the question: 'What tastes better?' I've found that this is a useful metaphor for every decision I have to make.

This was the wise advice of an American who has led the marketplace in developing and managing quality standards as a key figure in the Speciality Coffee Association of America and is currently a leading light in one of the US biggest quality roasters. He always talked about coffee clearly needing to taste good, but also needing to look good (we taste with our eyes), to feel and sound good too – perhaps the sound factor might be the barista saying 'Good Morning, Please or Thank You'. However, the price must taste good as well and whatever it is you are buying in whatever quantity, it must represent excellent value and leave you with that warm feeling that will make you come back for more.

Hugo true story – London railway station

On my way to a conference in London I was craving my caffeine hit and queued at a national chain for a cappuccino. Slowly I got to place my order, paid £2.40 and watched as the barista turned her back to me and proceeded to pull a single shot into a 12 oz cup (although I asked for a small cappuccino) and then left the steam wand texturing the milk in the jug as she unpacked more disposable lids. When the milk was properly burnt and steaming she whacked the drink together and, despite there being six people behind me in the queue, I politely asked her to remake it as the milk was burnt and it looked awful. She strutted back and this time paid more attention to the milk which was okay but she used the same coffee shot. This time on my refusal she argued with me that she hadn't used the same coffee shot, but as I removed the lid to show her, she turned away and started again. At this point I asked her for my £2.40 back and she, somewhat stunned, asked why?! I insisted on a refund and three of the six in the queue left with me after the show.

Quality, Value for Money, Experience, Referral, Speed, Delivery, Presentation, Credibility and Attitude were all desperately wrong here . . . I wrote an article on 'Rip off Coffee Britain' in the taxi but unfortunately without my coffee hit.

Hugo true story – The 10 oz 'Mervyn'

I recently advised one of my clients who needed a USP to sell his hero product with a coffee-to-go from his existing coffee shop business, but to avoid confusion and maintain speed, just do a 10 oz one-size option. This would ensure a great tasting drink because he could use a double shot and give good value, addressing the buoyant to-go marketplace. The problem arose when his disposable sales guy rang me to tell me that it was all wrong because all the other customers in the area sold 12 oz drinks. He felt that it was bad advice to do a 10 oz because the customers would be unhappy (presumably being used to 12 oz conditioning). This is a classic example of why you need to be very careful when listening to sales representatives. Often there is no consideration to the number one criteria – taste, no idea about USPs, no ability to consider the benefit of difference, and no concept of product development.

Hugo true story – Questions

Many years ago my great Italian equipment friend once said to me, after a full afternoon of intense debate on water brew temperatures where his latest model was not quite doing what it was supposed to be doing. I asked what I thought was a sensible question. 'Hugo, we like you . . . You ask a lot of good questions that show you have a good knowledge and a good understanding of this . . . and then you ask a stupid one!' Well it certainly brings you back to reality and injects humour into a situation that eases the whole atmosphere. He did it really well. But it also taught me in these early days that you can't ask enough questions.

Very often we feel afraid to ask so-called experts or sales people to fully explain what they are talking about, just like at school when sometimes you didn't put your hand up to ask a question for fear of looking stupid. But as an adult you need to get past this and keep digging and keep questioning. My view today is that very often the stupid questions are actually the best!

Emotionally engaging your consumer

Relationships are all about emotion and business is all about persuasion. To persuade is to sell. Salesmen in general tend to get a bad rap – but actually persuading and selling ideas is very important. The great leaders in the world today are those who can sell their ideas, and the ability to sell an idea is a great thing. The business of selling is a great business, and a useful business to be in and you do have to remember that you are in it!

People are now getting bored with the whole commoditisation of everything. Go to your local Tesco or Sainsbury's and get the same thing only a little bit better or worse. In the coffee business we have been fighting against commoditisation for years, with a lot of very ordinary and poor coffee being passed off as quality, and many top brands selling mediocre and, frankly, some very badly made coffee and claiming excellence.

Today's consumer wants to be emotionally engaged, they need to have a relationship. You have to deliver at that level. They need to trust you. That relationship, whether that's with an idea, a great cup of coffee, a delicious bun, excellent service or great value – if you don't give it to them, you're certainly never going to be able to charge a premium.

> **The essence of a great coffee experience is the perception in the minds of the consumer and your coffee experience has to look, feel, sound and smell fantastic too.**

Touch

- Is the cup comfortable?

- If disposable, does it have a suitable heat barrier or is it too hot because it is single walled? Do you need a jacket?

- Is it good quality? Do you trust it not to leak? Are lids available?

- If it is porcelain, is it big enough? Is it the right shape?

- Can you get your fingers in the handle easily?

- Does the saucer match? Is the spoon functional? Have you a doily?

- Is the furniture comfortable? Does the table wobble?

- Is it clean?

Sight

- Easy I know, but does the coffee look good? We taste with our eyes.

- Latte art? Good crema? Proper colour? Why not?

- Is the food offer aligned?

- Is the bun offer bountiful?

- Is the cup clean?

Sound

■ Did the service sound good? Did the staff say 'please' and 'thank you'?

■ Can you hear any music? If not do you have an ipod?

■ Can you hear the plane take off as your milk is textured?

■ Does it sound clean?

Taste

The obvious – but have you checked your coffee for temperature, body and flavour?

Perhaps you could go up a notch and consider sweetness, acidity, astringincy and bitterness. The next step is to analyse aromas as well as aftertaste, persistence, consistency and tactile balance. Too much detail? Not if you want to become a coffee expert. You are in the coffee business after all.

Is the taste clean?

Smell

Aroma experts say that one of the few smells that you cannot bottle is freshly roasted coffee. Our memories from our youth going to international rugby matches in Dublin is that anchored smell of Grafton Street where the famous Bewleys used to roast coffee in their shop. To this day that smell is still associated with Grafton Street to millions of people and demonstrates the potential power of the use of smell in branding.

Many large organisations have significantly invested in the smell of their environment. Think bookshops, sub-sandwich bars and perfume stores.

Is your coffee fresh? Does the food smell delicious? What do your toilets smell like?

Again, and importantly, does it smell clean?

Intuition matters

Our senses work together and when they are stimulated at the same time the results are unforgettable. And it is when the senses work together that you find the indefinable sixth sense we call intuition. Impossible to measure, it gets discounted from every business equation.

If your focus is on connecting with customers, then intuition matters.

We must create feeling and be emotional about what we are selling. It takes great partnerships with people who can help and support this process, because you can't do it all yourself – there are simply too many things that you need to be an expert at. If you have the right partners and you can model the right behaviours of big business, you can achieve amazing results.

So figure out how to stand out by applying sensuality to your business. Does that make sense?

3   Positioning

LOCATION, LOCATION, LOCATION IS . . . NONSENSE, NONSENSE, NONSENSE

This phrase is just a handy hook that's used by flash estate agents to try to convince you into high rent sites. It's also one of those clichés that is trotted out by accountants and people who really have no grasp of how this business works.

That's not to say that location doesn't matter – it does, but the more important concept is that of context and positioning and exactly what your offer can or should be. You really need to work out exactly what you're going to be and who you're going to appeal to before you even consider location. It's likely that you'll visit many sites as you consider opening your store that will be sold to you as 'perfect for a coffee shop'. This simply isn't true in each case. A site that may be perfect for a Starbucks is likely to be very different to that which is perfect for a very cosy food-driven coffee house.

Highly subjective Hugo and Johnny location fact number one

Whilst wandering down the 'main drag' of a large UK city one evening on a two-day 'gig' for a client, Hugo and I were looking for something to eat. It was about 8.00 p.m. and we passed somewhere in the region of 20 restaurants, most of which, if they weren't actual chains, were a classic 'me-too' offer, i.e. they simply looked at the chain model and decided 'we can do that just as well, if not better'.

The common factor with all of them though, was that they were on probably the highest rent street. Perhaps the guys at the 'good' end were paying a little more than the ones at the 'bad' end but, without a shadow of a doubt, they were paying top dollar to their landlords.

The second common factor with them all was that none of them appealed in ANY way to us. We weren't after a magnificent gastronomic experience, we just wanted something tasty in a relatively interesting environment, somewhere for us to mull over the days work and come out with our usual flashes of utter brilliance to astound the client with the next day.

The final common factor was that most of them were, at best, half full.

I vaguely remembered having eaten in this city before in a classic little Italian that was half way up a side street hill and down a few stairs. It was the sort of place that you could easily miss, but my recollection was based on the fact that it had served wonderful food, had an amazing atmosphere, but also so busy that we had been forced to perch at the counter and eat our food. The fact was that this hadn't made any difference to the experience. It hadn't put me off in any way, and to large extent, had actually made it a more fun experience.

The only problem was that I couldn't remember where this place was and had no idea of its name. We tentatively approached a taxi driver looking for any clues. I say tentatively because some taxi drivers seem to live in a parallel universe where it is okay to be quite staggeringly rude to the people who might give you money. On this occasion we got one of the good guys and I vaguely explained my memories of this place. He instantly knew where we were talking about and about five minutes later we were standing at the front door.

The place was heaving – we got great service, outstanding food and left happy with the world. Now on the commercial market the rent on this site would have been much less than half what the 'big boys' were paying on the high street. So not only were we happy but the owner was happy too, because such a tiny fraction of his turnover was going on rent.

Reasonable rent

It's also worth bearing in mind, because it's of *crucial* importance, that your rent is part of an overall equation. We'll deal with the specifics of this 'equation' later in the money section but at this stage you just need to grasp that your rent should be approximately 10% of your turnover (after VAT or local sales tax). But this is just a rule of thumb or a starting point. If you can get your rent below that level then every percent is another percent of net profit in your back pocket. Likewise, if it's above that then you need to make sure that you have enough gross margin to help compensate.

What do you want to offer?

We have two different clients both of whom are highly successful in their own right and both of whom occupy what would traditionally be regarded as poor sites. One of them is actually stuck way out in the country and only accessible by car. Both of them have rent percentages below 5% but they are highly food-driven 'destination-sites'. They have taken time to grow and have built up a reputation for great food and coffee in a relaxed and very different environment from the classic high street models. This creates a very loyal customer base that is likely to spend little or no time even entertaining the concept of visiting one of the big speciality coffee chains. Likewise the average Starbucks customer would find little appeal in either of our client's coffee shops. To a large extent their 'off the beaten track' location is actually an advantage.

So the key point is work out exactly what it is that you want to offer. If you're offering a sort of cool bohemian café, then ideally you'll need to be near a university or the creative part of a city. If you're creating perfect coffee and don't want to spend too much effort on food, then you will want to be in a small site in a large city near a train station. If you want a strongly food-lead offer, then you can allow yourself to be in a variety of different sites that may allow people to be in a more relaxed environment.

This concept leads clearly onto the notion of USP, or unique selling proposition. It's a classic sort of 'consultant' phrase to bandy around, but by giving it a bit of attention you may end up with a much clearer view of what your 'position' is within the market and the sorts of locations that might work for you.

Vastly less subjective Hugo and Johnny location factor number two

We have a client with a small chain of speciality coffee shops. The shops are generally located in good sites, but a few doors down or on the other side of the street from where the big boys operate. These sites are generally about 25% to 33% cheaper than what the large chains might be paying.

One of the sites sits a few doors down from one of the 'big three' in the UK. As an experiment we spent some time with a 'clicker' monitoring the traffic in and out of both the client's store and the chain store. After several days it transpired that our client was doing 40% more volume than the chain. Of course footfall doesn't take into account average spend and therefore doesn't accurately reflect into sales, so with some extreme craftiness we managed to 'discover' the sales for one day up to the same time of day. The 40% rule continued to apply and clearly the fact that the chain, with the better stand and the huge UK wide media presence, were taking absolutely no advantage from their better location.

So what was the factor? Well it may come as no surprise to you that our client was offering better coffee, better service and better food. Sometimes this business isn't actually rocket science. But the key issue is that he didn't just *think* he was offering a better version of the chain (which a lot of operators do think) – he actually WAS and he spent pretty much every hour of every day making sure that that continued to be the case. This client, a little like Gordon Ramsay advocates, refused to listen to any positive comments and only focused on the complaints and the negatives so that there was no sense of allowing himself to have smoke blown up his backside.

Again – there's a lesson there.

NOMENCLATURE

It's very important once you make the transition from being an owner operator to becoming a fancy consultant and speaker about a subject to make sure you use poncy language. Therefore when discussing the naming of your business (or indeed your 'brand'), you do not call it 'naming' you call it 'nomenclature'. This helps you to justify charging larger fees for what you do.

Having said that, nomenclature isn't actually just the creation of the name for your business it's actually an incredibly important consideration. It really does need some thought and you need to go into the process with a clear idea of what you want from it and, almost more importantly, no strict adherence to a name that may have been kicking around your mind for years in a 'when I open my coffee bar I'm going to call it Jimmy after my first teddy bear' fashion.

It's crucial that your name covers two key points.

1. It's memorable.

2. It must not be confusing and ideally manage to incorporate coffee or some coffee aspect into it.

It should be relatively short and in an ideal world only one or two words long. Let's consider some of the biggest coffee (and coffee related) brands in the world.

- Starbucks
- Subway
- Costa Coffee
- Caffe Nero
- Coffee Bean and Tea Leaf
- Coffee Beanery
- Dunkin Donuts
- Tim Horton's
- Caribou Coffee
- Peet's Coffee

What we generally see is the use of one name that the business is identified by and then often 'coffee' attached in some form. There is a tremendous amount to be said for this and for not being too 'clever' with your name. Most operators assume that the passing general public will know what they are doing by the look of the shop but you would be amazed at just how often this isn't the case.

There are a variety of coffee associated terms that can be used but again you need to exercise caution since they will have very different perceptions in the mind of the customer. 'Roast' has generally good images in the mind of the customer and 'bean' can also be used successfully. 'Grind' has too much of a negative image in the mind of many customers and conjures up images of the daily 'grind' of commuting or their jobs, which is everything that your coffee bar should be trying to escape from. So beware of 'hilarious' pun driven names like 'The Daily Grind' or 'Nose to the Grindstone'. In fact, beware of names that are puns full stop. They are rarely funny in any way after about ten minutes of use. 'Bean there, done that'?

'Filter', 'brew' and other associated terms are somewhat clinical terms too that you need to be careful with.

The use of two words, one of which is coffee and the other one interesting and ideally memorable, is hard to beat and coupled with a decent strapline (ideally no more than four words long) can provide you with clarity, something that can be easily understood. Straplines need to try to expand on what you're doing without narrowing the niche too much.

'Passionate about coffee', 'religious about coffee', 'coffee is our passion', 'great food, great coffee', 'Ireland's best coffee', 'truly outstanding coffee', all help to reinforce the fact that you really care about coffee. The problem here is that the name is defined by your model and vice versa. So are you a coffee shop, coffee house, café, café/restaurant, coffee bar? How much of your turnover will be purely coffee driven?

For example, if you adopt a name like:

Hector's Coffee
Coffee is our passion

you're pretty much nailing your allegiances to the coffee mast. If, however, you expect and hope for a big lunch trade and perhaps want to open a couple of nights for dinner too then you may be better advised to do something like:

Hector's House
Restaurant/coffee house

It's not clever or funny but it is a very clear statement about what you do. By referring to yourself as a coffee house and restaurant, you don't intimidate those people who just want a coffee and happen to be walking past and see your sign, and likewise you'll help alert people to the fact that you are more than just an espresso bar and that food is a major part of your offer.

So keep it simple, make it memorable and ensure that you have as much information contained in the name and any tag line as possible.

POSITIONING

Positioning is about making sure that everything you do matches up with the end consumer. That means everything. When you're creating your business you need to think about keeping the following items consistent and coherent with what your market will want. You'll need to use the 'Bob and Brenda' technique in the people section to get this completely right, but with this customer avatar in your mind you can, in addition to your location and name, clearly look at:

- **Signage** – how brash can you be? Will it jar with the customers? How can you make it as obvious as possible without offending?
- **Menu creation** – how does it flow throughout the day? How does it match or conflict with your competitors?
- **Staffing** – attitudes, style, education?
- **Uniforms** – will they be formal, cool, casual, relaxed?
- **Pricing** – you must be as brave as you can but can't price yourself out of the market.
- **Furniture** – will it encourage people to stay and lounge? Do you want that?
- **Marketing** – how will you get hold of your target market? What messages will they want to hear? What will turn them off?
- **Merchandising** – how can you position products to sell best?

4 People

Now that we've established that you need great passion to get started and that this passion has produced a great product, we need to focus, and that means really focus, on the people side of things. Understanding people and how they work is the key skill. This includes customers and staff. This means doing extensive work on how to hire, train and retain great staff, and extensive work on the concept of 'customer shoes' and the psychology behind that.

Hopefully we've now made it crystal clear that you're not going to either hide yourself away at the back barking orders or do everything on your own muttering quietly under your breath 'if you want a job done properly you'd better do it yourself'.

An essential, and occasionally infuriating, truism about business is that no matter how good your product is or how great a location you have, unless you can fully understand people and how they work, your business simply won't succeed. And that means an understanding of all people that you come into contact with – customers, suppliers, staff, bankers, partners etc. You will need to learn how to manage all of these individual groups effectively, so that your business can reach the potential objective that you laid out so clearly when deciding what you wanted from it (begin with the end in mind).

Our experience and understanding of how to grow and develop business has come though a variety of sources. We both sat through (and if we're honest largely ignored like the rest of the class) the 'people' parts of our degrees. At the age of 20, filled with great ideas and bravado, you can find vastly more interesting things to do than mulling over the intricacies of Maslow's Heirarchy of Needs and trying to remember exactly what 'self-actualization' means. Our priorities lay in the slightly less esoteric pleasures of girls and beer, which may not ultimately have been a bad thing.

Real understanding of people and how they work and behave hits you like a brick when you open your first business – particularly within the hospitality or catering arena. Suddenly grand theoretical notions of how to motivate staff fly out the window when you're faced with a group of employees earning a couple of pounds an hour with about as much interest in your passion and vision that you might have in the inner workings of an abattoir.

So once you have set your grand notions to one side you can quickly (and usually painfully) recalibrate and work out exactly how you are going to get people to buy in to what you want to do as well as persuading customers that what you do is a great thing. Between us in the past 20 years we have recruited and employed in excess of 500 members of staff. We have operated businesses in markets and industries far outside of coffee shops, in areas such as classic retail, distribution, marketing services, the internet (somewhat disastrously it has to be said) as well as the obvious and oft-mentioned chip shops and restaurant sectors.

In our consultancy business we have worked with clients with hundreds of employees and spend hours developing recruitment, training and development programs that particularly resonate with employees in the coffee shop business. We do a lot of video training and analysis and have spent hundreds of hours, with and without clients, pouring over videos of busy coffee shops to observe how staff and customers behave at different times of the day and in varying circumstances. This is occasionally tedious but most of the time utterly fascinating and with some fairly elementary understandings of body language, tone and facial expressions, you really can unlock the keys to how people behave and what they ideally want both as an employee and a customer.

We say all this not in a sense of 'look at us, aren't we brilliant' attitude, but to emphasise just how deep we go in terms of understanding people within a coffee shop scenario and how incredibly important it is for you to apply some of these lessons even before you open the till on day one of trading in your shiny new coffee shop. We also emphasise it to illustrate that our one big theory that came off the back of this research and experience was backed up by a hell of a lot more than just a fancy MBA and reading a lot of books.

The key concept that comes out of this, and which you can directly apply to all your dealings with people in your new business can be summarised by two words. Or more specifically two names: Bob and Brenda.

BOB AND BRENDA; UNDERSTANDING HOW CUSTOMERS THINK

Bob and Brenda are the result of the creation of what we term as a customer 'avatar'. Initially the process was created as a way to really understand how customers think (and therefore craft the business around that) but it has since spread into every interaction that we have with people.

The following quote from Peter Drucker – arguably the greatest management thinker of the twentieth century – is just one of a variety of sources that led us towards the creation of this concept.

The aim of marketing is to know and understand the customer so well the product or service fits him and sells itself.

It's this really deep understanding of how a customer thinks and feels that is incredibly powerful. It's also something that is incredibly difficult to do when you are immersed in the day-to-day management of your business. Throughout our careers, both with clients and our own staff, we have constantly advocated the process of looking at things through 'customer eyes' or walking the store in 'customer shoes', but the reality is that this isn't anything like as easy to do as it sounds.

What you'll find is that as you move from being a customer in other people's coffee shops to actually operating your own, your entire emphasis will shift. Even if you aren't consciously aware of it, you will gradually see everything from an operator's perspective and start to ignore those things that customers see. It doesn't apply in all situations obviously – a dirty toilet, messy table or obviously poor service will still annoy you as much as ever, but your ability to perceive small irritations will gradually reduce as you become obsessed with things on the employee side of the counter.

This is human nature and it's actually a process that we have to learn. There are numerous scientific examples which help to illustrate this (visit www.freecoffeeboys.com for more examples) but one of the best was an experiment where a child of three is handed a cube with one side painted green. The other five sides are left white. The child is clearly shown that the cube has only one green side and that from other sides it will appear to be white.

The cube is then positioned between the child and another person with the green side facing the child. The child is asked what colour the cube is. Naturally since he sees the green he replies that it is green. He is then asked what colour the other person thinks the cube is. Even though he knows that the cube has white on all other faces he will still reply that the other person will think it is green. Since what he sees is a green cube, he cannot imagine that the other person sees anything differently.

If you do the same experiment with a five or six year old they can start to see the cube from the other person's perspective and will answer that they will think it is white.

The problem with this is that we obviously do manage to see things from another person's perspective in isolation when presented with simple objects like a cube, but in day-to-day life we can be just as blinkered as the three year old insisting that the cube is green. We tend to go through life in a trance, particularly in situations that we're very familiar with. If we have a reasonable commute to work in the mornings we are all familiar with the concept that huge stretches of the journey simply cannot be remembered and we wonder exactly how we could be so 'switched off' and not crash the car. In a working environment it is exactly the same. We come in and work to a large extent on autopilot, oblivious to everyone and everything around us, purely concentrating on those things that we perceive to be important. We may still have conversations with people but we're a heck of a long way off being able to see things from the perspective of another person unless we very consciously do so.

Without becoming too esoteric this ties in very strongly with what the poet Keats calls the 'negative capability'. This is the process where we can remove our intellectual selves from the process of reading or writing and see it from another perspective. In the case of our writing this is very important. We have to shift between a number of different modes when we write since we have a variety of distinctly different audiences that we appeal to. This book is ostensibly aimed at people who have yet to open a coffee shop and yet we still need to provide value to those people who have opened a shop and are looking for further advice. Our previous book *Wake Up and Smell the Profit: 52 Guaranteed Ways to Make More Money in Your Coffee Business* is, as the title clearly suggests written for people who already own a shop. If we wrote this book in the same manner as the first book we would clearly irritate those readers who have yet to open their shop and may be unfamiliar with some coffee shop jargon. In an ideal world we would like both sets of readers to read both books, but the really critical point is that you cannot expect to be all things to everyone, i.e. you must nail your colours to the mast and primarily aim at one audience. If other people like that as well then that's great, but it should never be your primary focus.

The implications of this in terms of your new coffee shop (or existing one if you happen to be reading from that perspective) are obviously huge. What you have to do is get right into the head of your customer and see what is going on. Your offer and marketing needs to be directed at that specific market and not driven purely by what you think would be a great idea. When you *really* understand how the customer thinks, acts, feels and what their needs are, you can create products that really appeal to them at a very deep level.

If you can properly put yourself in your customer's shoes you can start to see all the strange conversations that we (and they) have with ourselves. Ultimately most of what we look like and say externally is a front. It's a rational representation of the person we would like to be. At heart though we are filled with incredibly irrational frustrations and fears. If you can get so deep into the mind of your customer (and later your staff) that you can listen to these conversations, then you really have cracked the code in terms of being able to provide what they really want.

So how do we understand how customers think?

You take time, real time to observe, talk and think about who these customers are and exactly what they might feel at each stage in your business. You think really hard about the conversations and insecurities that you have when you visit coffee shops, restaurants or retail outlets. You think about how often you are made to feel foolish or confused and how much you hate it.

But this takes time – proper reflective time. As business folk we tend to be constantly, restlessly busy. The big problem with having the entrepreneurial or even managerial mindset is that we all like to get stuff done. Getting stuff done is always a laudable goal, but it also makes it extremely difficult to be the type of person who sits back and observes. The other problem with this is that when we sit in our own businesses we do the 'owner shuffle' which is that cross, frustrated wriggling around in the seat that we do when we see a customer being ignored or an employee doing something they shouldn't be doing, i.e. we always want to be fixing stuff.

> **The way we do this, for our own businesses or for clients, is to spend a lot of time watching customers in action.**

You need to sit back and watch (really watch) customers for hours either in other coffee shops or your own if you've already taken the leap. If you do already have a coffee shop you need to record videos of how they behave at all the key points in the process.

Observing customer behaviour

Here are a few key areas that you need to observe about customers:

■ Watch them as they come to the door – is the signage clear? Are they confused with the push or pull of the door?

■ Watch as they enter and as they approach the counter. Do they know where to go? Do they pause and look awkward?

■ Watch to see if they're confused and wonder if it is counter service or table service.

■ If you're in a counter service shop, watch to see how they peruse the food on sale stock. Do they look enticed? Do they 'oooh and ahhhh' and adopt a 'I deserve a little treat and that's too delicious to ignore' face? Or do they have a dismissive look on their face and are clearly not tempted?

■ How do they react to a greeting from the counter staff? Do they get a pleasant greeting at all?

■ How does their body language alter as they move through the queue? Are they comfortable or stiff?

■ Are they being upsold to (in a 'would you like to go large?' fashion), and if so, how does this shift their body language and facial expressions?

■ What happens when they have placed their order? Are they confused or do they know what to do? Are they given clear instructions about collecting their drinks or food?

■ How do regular customers behave in comparison to new customers?

■ How do they behave after purchase? Do they easily find a seat? Do they easily find any condiments they need?

■ What about those people who need to use the toilet? Is it easy for them to find it? Do they shuffle around in a lost fashion and then pluck up the courage to ask or is it clear?

■ What is their facial expression after they leave the toilet? Is it 'Bloody hell, I'm never venturing in there again' or 'That was okay actually'?

This list can be endless. The point is that you need to really observe every intricate detail of how people behave so that you can create the image in your mind of what is important and what isn't for a customer. We cannot emphasise how crucial this is as an exercise.

What is the customer thinking?

You must make endless notes too. You're trying to help create the picture in your mind of exactly what the customer is thinking. And again make sure you don't forget that these thoughts are not rational. We all bounce around the day with our mind filled with irrational thoughts. It's the sheer irrationality of these thoughts and your ability to tap into them that can allow you to really get inside their heads and then really tailor everything you do towards them.

What you'll also grasp quite quickly is that customers generally don't want to interact with businesses they want to interact with people. They're not thinking about your business they're thinking about the people in it at that time and what they're doing or not doing for them. When they're in your shop your brand, or fancy adverts don't matter a jot to them. All that matters are the people who are actually serving them and creating the experience for them.

This process is very difficult for many operators to fully grasp. We are, as a nation, wary of emotions and the irrationality that exists within us, so exercises like this can tend to be quite difficult. Our 'stiff upper lip' tends to preclude us from being able to dig deep into our own emotions let alone those of our customers. To help with this it's useful (with staff or partners) to extrapolate and imagine what might have happened to key individuals that you may be observing before they arrive.

The pre-work cup of coffee is always a good place to start. Most people are a little late, a little grumpy and really not quite awake as they arrive into your shop in the morning. By the very definition of your shop, i.e. a 'coffee' shop, we have to assume that they quite badly need a caffeine hit. We can also start to imagine what their journey into work was like. All forms of transport are pretty horrendous these days so not only are they likely to be suffering from caffeine withdrawals but they're also extremely likely to be harassed after their journey.

■ How many of us sit up a little late the previous night watching a movie when we know we should be in bed?

■ How many of us perhaps have an extra glass of wine which may just take the edge off the morning?

- How many of us are 100% prepared for the early morning progress meetings?

- How many of us may leave the house after a row with a spouse or teenage child?

- How many people live alone (increasing numbers all the time) and have yet to hear a friendly voice that morning?

Some of these factors are highly likely to affect our theoretical early morning customers and a few hours spent observing them over a few days will help you see this etched on people's faces – not the face that they have when they order the drink, but the face they have when they think that nobody is watching them.

With these sorts of questions in mind we can then start to sit down and imagine what a conversation might be that goes on in the mind of a typical customer at this time. Again this is tricky for many of us and we come up with generic responses like:

'He's late for work and in a rush. He wants to get a cup of coffee quickly and something nice to eat so that he can get into work quickly.'

But the problem is that isn't enough. That's just a cliché. It's kind of what we all might say. It's safe. But to get to the full extent of this and get the true value out of it you must go deeper. When you go deep (just like when you go really deep into any part of your business) the real magic happens.

So what we really want is this – because this (and thoughts like this) are real life!

'I'm late and I really don't feel great. I wish I hadn't had that second glass of wine last night. I really regret not doing that extra work on my report before this meeting and I'm going to end up being made a fool out of by my boss again! The bus driver is an ignorant sod and I hope that girl from the shop up the road is in – I think I got my timings right.'

Obviously that is a slight exaggeration and that kind of model won't apply to every business but getting that deep into the mind of a customer allows you to see all those strange irrational ideas that constantly float around inside our heads rather than the 'together' image we portray to the outside world.

What you also get to see is a much better idea of what this customer might want to see when he arrives into your store at 8.25 a.m. trying to grab a quick coffee.

It shows how incredibly important remembering his name is. It shows just how important it is that you don't allow any 'Oh, I'm not a morning person' moaners to work behind your counter.

Creating an avatar

So using the Bob and Brenda model is about the creation of all of these people in a virtual form. It's about taking all these individual characters at each time of the day, creating an avatar that represents them and then naming it. An avatar is a term that is in common use on the internet – generally it is an exaggerated or slightly caricatured version of someone that is used for various social networking sites. What we're trying to do here is to establish an avatar that represents our ideal customers. To a large extent your customer avatar involves metaphorically taking all these ideal customers and putting them in a huge blender. If you can ignore the faintly disgusting notion of blending them all up, then the end result is your average customer.

So really getting on top of your avatar is crucial. But in our business (the coffee shop business) we need to look at a variety of avatars. The customer avatar buying his (or her) cup of coffee on the way to work is very different from the avatar of the mother arriving with a child in a push chair and hoping for a few moments of peace and sanity with her friends before she returns to pick up her older child from the nursery. Her irrational internal conversations will be very different, but it is just as important to get deep into her mindset if you want to keep her happy too.

Bear in mind again that this is NOT about being all things to all people. It is not about bending over backwards to accommodate all potential customers. Many of our clients simply don't want the mother and push chair crowd. They can be very difficult, demanding and annoying to other customers. But if you do want them then you must get in their minds to understand what they're thinking.

Naming an avatar

Once you have created your various avatars for the various times of day you then need to name them. Bob and Brenda are historically our lunchtime customer avatars. They vary from business to business obviously, but their names just seem to have stuck. You can create your own names of course, but it's useful to choose names that are a little tiny bit different or humorous because the next stage of this process is to translate it to your team.

Everything that you have just been through to understand your customers, must now extend to your staff because it needs to become a perpetual attitude within the business. The reality is that if your staff can always be thinking 'what would Bob and Brenda be thinking now?' then they're constantly thinking like a customer. They start to become much more aware of unclear merchandising and poor customer flow. They start to grasp how confusing menus can be and how an overly complex display can actually put people off. They start to see how fancy or 'hilarious' names for drinks can actually make them feel foolish. They start to grasp that the rules change during the day. They see that 'Derek' the early morning avatar has different needs from 'Daphne' who is a mid-morning customer. They stop the rigid following of rules and start to grasp that it's all about keeping these characters happy and seeing the shop from their perspective. They start to realise that a new customer is a very different beast, from a behavioural perspective, to an existing one.

When you're in the store you want to be constantly asking questions like:

'What would Bob and Brenda think of that?'

'Would that signage be confusing to Bob and Brenda?'

'If Bob came here every day what would start to irritate him?'

'What would Brenda want to eat on a Monday which might be different from a Friday?'

If you can keep asking these questions it becomes the mindset of the business. A simple look is all it needs before a member of staff says 'yes, I know – Bob wouldn't like that' and then they change it. The whole shift of the business moves away from being about what we want and think and towards what the customer wants and thinks.

When this happens you genuinely do end up with something magical and a quite enormously different perspective to that which exists within other businesses. If you can craft your new business with this in mind from day one – and indeed even before day one – then you have a huge advantage.

But as we explained earlier this is just one stage of the whole process. Once you have understood how the concept works from a customer perspective, you can then apply it towards all the other people that you need to deal with.

One of the eternal frustrations that you will learn is that bankers and other investors really don't care about anything that we care about. Over the years, both for our own businesses and for clients, we have produced beautiful reports and plans and presented them with a flourish to odd little bank managers sat in odd little offices in suits that don't really fit them. Every time what they do is take the report and flick to the back to look at the cashflow and capital requirements. They completely dismiss all the work and fancy graphs in the earlier part of the report.

But when you fully grasp the Bob and Brenda concept, you realise that of course this is the case. Why should they be bothered with what we are bothered with? Their criteria are radically different to ours. So with this in mind you can change your whole perspective (and the way you write reports).

Hugo true story – Humour and language

One of my best customers, who has since sold up and emigrated, was Northern Ireland's top publican for many years. He had a fantastic ability to use humour and language to build rapport and achieve his objectives. He used to call people, quite often very serious people, 'Big Lad', as in the Belfast vernacular. The look of surprise on their faces often changed the atmosphere and caused people to smile, creating the perfect state to get down to business. I have always believed that if you can make them laugh you can make them buy, and the power of humour, properly executed, can never be lost in any of our businesses. Try it with your customers, carefully, and they will want to return.

Slightly embarrassing Johnny true story

The Bob and Brenda concept came from a variety of different sources, many of whom were, like the great Peter Drucker, highly respected management thinkers. But one of the real clues for me came out of a slightly embarrassing phobia I had a few years ago. We live in an old house and one of the key issues of old houses is that they aren't exactly air tight, and since our house seems to have had a quite remarkable amount of bits added on and extended over the years, there have inevitably been created a few holes that small furry animals can get into.

So a few years ago we had a mouse problem. My daughter was very small and as she and I sat in our main living room a huge mouse (more like a small donkey to be honest) bounded through the room and into a little hole that it had found behind the TV. My daughter totally and utterly freaked out and so I relentlessly pursued him and disappeared out the window as my paternal macho tendencies leapt to the fore.

Over the next few weeks we discovered that our little donkey-sized friend was not alone. He had clearly worked hard on his marketing and had sent out great offers to all his friends in the neighbourhood. We caught loads of the wee b*****ds and after one particularly demented session in the spare room where I was acting like Jack Nicholson in The Shining, I realised that these wee fellas were really starting to get to me.

Eventually we got rid of them but by then my every waking (and some sleeping) hours seemed to be occupied with visions of little mice moving in my peripheral vision. If I was out for a walk and a leaf moved slightly in the wind I assumed it was a mouse. I would lie in bed at night imagining them crawling over the sheets and sometimes waken up ranting and raving like an idiot thinking that one had run across my face. Not good. I couldn't get the image of mice out of my mind so decided as a last resort to dig out the yellow pages and look for help from a hypnotist.

In an ideal world I wanted someone to do a faintly freaky 'look into my eyes, not around my eyes, but into my eyes . . .' session and five minutes later I'd wake up with no fear of mice and a nice warm glow about me. But hypnosis I discovered doesn't really work like that. What the hypnotist did was to take me into a very relaxed state and then make me imagine that there was a tiny little mouse (not one of our donkey-sized ones) in front of me looking up at me. He then made me disassociate myself from my body and imagine what the mouse would be thinking as it looked up at me. It was a somewhat surreal experience and I can still remember the terror that I could imagine the mouse feeling as I bore down on it.

Very quickly this process removed all my fear of mice and I was able to get perspective back into the situation. But what really stuck with me was how powerful the feeling was of seeing everything from someone else's eyes.

The Bob and Brenda concept can be taken much, much deeper than we've taken it here, but what I tend to do now when I'm observing customer behaviour on behalf of a client, is to attempt to get back into this state and actually see everything through the eyes of the customer I'm observing.

When writing or speaking from the stage I also try to 'flip' myself into the position of the reader or the audience. When you can position yourself properly in this way it fundamentally changes how you write and speak. So once more – please don't underestimate how important this process is when you're putting together your business.

DEALING WITH EMPLOYEES

The other major group of people that you need to deal with in your business is your employees. Call them what you will – staff, employees, team members, colleagues or whatever the current fashionable jargon is, but one fact remains. If you can't get them on your side and wanting to work for you, then you're really going to struggle with your new business.

Employing people is tough – no doubt about it. And increasingly you need to be very wary of legislation and make sure you stay within the law during the whole process, right until you finally bid a fond farewell to a great employee, or an exasperated 'thank goodness for that' when you finally get rid of a terrible hiring mistake.

The concept of Bob and Brenda is hugely important here too and it applies even before you open the doors. If you're going to attract the best staff you need to work out exactly where they might be now and also how you're going to persuade them that your shop will be the best place to work. This again is where most new (and existing) operators fall down. They create a recruitment process that is almost exactly the same as their competitors. For most people who operate a coffee shop that involves one of three options.

1. Stick an ad in the local paper.

2. Stick a sheet of A4 in the window with 'STAFF WANTED – APPLY WITHIN' written on it.

3. Ask existing staff if they know anyone who may be able to help.

That's it. Ninety-five percent of owners adopt those three 'recruitment processes' and generally as their first option just stick with one. Now, is it any surprise that at least 80% of owners (and yes we have surveyed this) would regard 'getting decent staff' as one of their top three problems? Many actually regard the effective staffing of their establishments as the number one problem that their business has.

The concept behind '52 ways . . .' and how you can apply it not just to recruitment but to every aspect of your business

When we wrote our first book, the '52 ways' title was almost as important as the content. The content was effectively a distillation of many of our conversations over the previous ten years about what had worked or hadn't worked with our clients or our own businesses. But behind that was the issue of trying to change mindsets within the coffee shop community. Where a Formula One team thrives and is driven by relentless improvement and innovation, many coffee shop operators are incredibly stuck in their ways.

The '52 ways' was a development of a concept and a conversation that we had with a client who was struggling to make more money in his business. We knew he was actually doing very little about it and was more content to moan and look for excuses rather than actually try something new, so we decided to test him a little in a faintly confrontational way.

We sat down with him and said we would help out. What we wanted to know before we began though was what he had already tried so that we didn't have any crossover, and perhaps see if we could tweak what he had already tried to make it work.

With a fresh notebook in front of us and our pens poised we said to him:

'Let's see what we can do here, can you list off the last 50 things that you've done to try and increase profits?'

Dumbfounded he looked at us and replied:

'Well obviously I haven't tried 50 things, that would be ridiculous.'

'Okay, no problem' we replied 'what about the last twenty?'

'Well I haven't done twenty either' he retorted, in a quite irritated tone.

'Fine, no problem' we carried on, without obviously passing judgement, 'just give us the last ten.'

Somewhat exasperated he replied 'I haven't done ten things either, I don't know how many I've done.'

'Five? Four? Three? . . .' we quizzed.

It turned out that he'd tried two things. He had put one terrible ad in the local paper which was deservedly ignored and he'd tweaked his lunchtime menu to create some more value-driven options.

But the message had been made clear. He actually hadn't really tried anything. He was simply expecting to open the doors in the morning and make money.

It was this conversation that sparked the book off. It became a challenge to come up with 50 ideas ourselves and then turn it into a convenient 52, or one a week. We actually ended up with well over a hundred which had to be whittled down, so maybe at some stage we'll do a '52 ways – Part II – The Revenge'.

A year or so later we were in the same situation with another client who was really struggling to get staff. The same exercise produced a similar response – except they were actually only doing one basic thing to get new staff. We rattled off about 50 different solutions for recruitment to prove that there can and should be better ways to get great staff together.

RECRUITING GREAT STAFF

The recruitment of great staff for your new team needs to be a lot more creative than just relying on the three ways described above. The key thing is to effectively always be recruiting. We've found that the very best entrepreneurial coffee shop owners never switch off in their hunt for great staff. They're always on the lookout in restaurants and bars for staff who could fit the profile of their ideal employee avatar and will brazenly approach people to come and work for them. Most great employees are underappreciated so very often this method can be very successful.

You need to do the same – long before you have ever opened the doors. You need to be creating an image in your mind of your employee avatar and be constantly searching for people who fit that mode. Your initial recruitment should also involve an ad campaign in the local paper and a large poster on the window. To attract the best staff you will need to be bold and confident in your approach and structure your approach to what would appeal to them.

You need to sit down and work out exactly what goes on in the mind of a great barista or coffee shop employee. If you currently work in the business, ask your friends and colleagues what would appeal to them in a job. It may well be different from what you're thinking. One of the great things that Starbucks did was to offer free health care to employees who worked over a certain amount of hours per week. With health care costs so prohibitive in the US this was of huge appeal to potential new staff. They also, in the early days at least, appeared to be a 'cool' place to work. Why work in a smelly old café or chip shop when you could be part of a 'Third Place'? Those two factors were a killer blow in terms of getting people to want to work for them, and that is the ultimate goal out of all of this – not to be always looking for new staff, but to have a list of people queuing up and waiting for a job.

Another client of ours has a wonderful little coffee shop in a pleasant town. They recruit a lot of girls and boys from the local school, but because they have positioned the business in a certain way the parents of the children regard it as a wonderful place for their precious little lambs to start their working career. This means they have a huge supply of people always wanting to work for them.

Ideally you must find your own competitive advantage, but again it boils down to establishing the avatar and then creating the job and perks around that. Once you have established this it's a relatively simple process to craft your advertisements and posters to appeal to these people.

APPLICATION FORMS

As mentioned at the beginning, this book is not about providing details of exact wording of application forms and such like. What it is about is helping you to think in a certain way that will radically increase your chances of success. One of those ways is categorically NOT to have an application form like everyone else. Therefore you need to inject some personality into the form. Your basic form needs to have all the legal requirements (see the Federation of Small Businesses (FSB) or your solicitor for this), and you obviously need to avoid the usual stuff like asking prospective employees if they're pregnant or what their religion is – but beyond that, you have a fairly blank canvas (regardless of what human resource professionals may tell you).

The key thing is to weed out as many people as possible who won't fit your avatar. Interviewing useless boring staff is one of the greatest wastes of your time and needs to be avoided at all costs. A good application form will help you avoid some of this.

Be aware that most people lie on their application forms. Not everyone produces great big whopping lies about degrees or work experience, but most people exaggerate their character somewhat and try to slot in a few hobbies that really don't exist. Most people have an auto-pilot application filling-in process that they simply switch on when they're filling in a form. Since form filling is one of the most tedious exercises known to mankind, it's hard to blame them.

Your form needs to shock them out of this state and also help show a little personality. If you operate your store in a bookshop you probably want relatively well-read employees who can empathise with the customer and would, in certain situations, regard working in a bookshop as an ideal job. So instead of asking them to list out their hobbies, ask them to write a single paragraph about their favourite book. This will be a great opportunity for your avatar and will put off those folk who see it as 'just another job'. This strategy can be used for films, music or anything else that you feel might appeal to what you are trying to create within your shop. Why not ask them about the best meal they ever had if you're a very food-driven site, or the best coffee they had if you strive for the best coffee in the country.

The hidden advantage of this approach is that it generates word of mouth – an interesting and different application form (as long as it's not a pain to fill out) is a great way to get the potential employees who match your avatar to start chattering to each other about your business, and that's always good and always more effective than countless adverts in the papers. Even if you don't ask anything innovative, you MUST have a section where you ask why they want to work for you. If the answers are generic nonsense like 'it's on my bus route' or 'I need the money', you then have a great excuse for chucking the form in the bin.

Hugo true story – Choosing baristas

In our business we have recruited, trained and coached hundreds of baristas. I always think an interesting fact is that the really good ones are reasonably easily spotted at the start. This is because they are the ones with the best attitudes.

Clearly people are very different with varied strengths and weaknesses. Some come along with some good skills and many talk about their excellent coffee knowledge and experience working for a chain, or of having completed specific training that they think will be very useful. While this can help the business at the start they are usually always the people that don't work out.

When we are recruiting for a new project we always look for people who have a good attitude. Skill can come from knowledge and we can give them lots of knowledge, although I accept that this can take time. The overall key factor that makes the recruiting job easier is that they come with the right attitude. A 'can do', positive and disciplined approach will always bear fruit and the business can be massively rewarded by investing in training this person.

Needless to say we always look for people who 'give a s*it' and they are easier than you think to spot. We just spend a bit more time finding them and don't hire if we are in any doubt.

THE INTERVIEW

Once you have selected your shortlist you need to phone the candidates and see if they're available for an interview. The key thing here is, unless you have a highly trained and effective PA (and let's assume you don't), you should phone them yourself and conduct a mini-interview. You're wasting your time and theirs if you invite a grunting buffoon with a decent application form along for an interview just because you were too polite to say 'No way . . . !' after they answer the phone sounding like a cross between an elephant and the famous teenage character Kevin played by Harry Enfield.

The trick is to ask if you can go through a couple of things on the application form. Ask them to confirm that they're still interested in the job and how quickly would they be available for interview if they were selected. Query a couple more items on the form and if they sound as if they might be half decent you can then offer an interview. If they sound useless then you can simply thank them for there time and say you'll get back to them if you want to interview them.

The actual interview itself is something that is criminally messed up by many owners. For some reason they seem to enjoy the torture of sitting through interviews and asking every available question.

Johnny true story – Fast walkers

In my last trading business we had in excess of 100 employees spread over a number of different locations. I managed 90% of the recruitment and, since the business was quite seasonal and there was a fairly high turnover of staff, I did a lot of interviews myself. By this stage I had already employed a lot of people but it was here that I really refined my interviewing skills and understanding of body language and how to read it. Hugh and I have a full one-day course to help managers understand and read body language, but there was one particular thing that I learnt in this business that helps to short cut any interviewing process you may have for retail or catering jobs.

My office was situated about 150 yards from the main reception area. Out of politeness and to avoid being seen as a big intimidating boss (which never helps in terms of getting the best out of a candidate), I used to walk across to reception to meet the candidate and engage in a little small talk as we walked back to the office. What I was really doing was trying to grasp how well they could speak to me in a pleasant and articulate manner without the constraints of an office or the application form. I wanted to see how the conversation would ebb and flow as I asked the usual guff about the weather or how they had travelled to the interview. Obviously if they spoke confidently that helped enormously, and if they could make me laugh and entertain me they went up a huge notch since nearly all our jobs were customer facing.

I'm one of those annoying people who walks far too fast, so I quickly noticed that the keen ones would keep up and adapt their walking to me rather than hanging back and forcing me to walk at their pace. The ones who hung back like Brian the Snail and walked at their own pace would, almost without exception, turn out to be rubbish interviewees. So 'the walk' became one of my major criteria and wherever we travel Hugh and I talk about whether staff in coffee shops or restaurants are slow or fast walkers. Pretty much almost without exception you'll find that the fast walkers provide great service and the slow walkers provide rubbish service.

The point of this is not to tell some fatuous story about how to judge people by how fast they walk, but to show how much you need to absorb and pay attention to other factors aside from the classic questions and answers on an application form, and lines that have been rehearsed in front of the mirror at home.

Interview techniques

Standard interview techniques will involve being very thorough and checking off boxes. It's easy to become paralysed by the process and ultimately end up with rubbish staff simply because you haven't really worked out properly whether they will be good or not in your situation. Unfortunately the ability to interview well (and not waste lots of your time) is hard to learn from a book, but here are a few key things to bear in mind.

■ Gut feeling. Again we can hear every HR professional and a few lawyers up and down the land raising their eyebrows to this one, but it is of huge importance. Your gut feeling is rarely wrong and you should learn to trust it when interviewing.

■ If they're late ask them why in a relatively confrontational manner – 90% of the time you simply won't employ someone who cannot bother to turn up to an interview on time but a good candidate, with a genuine reason for being late, can shine in a situation like this.

■ Immediately mentally position them in your coffee shop or kitchen and see if you can get them to 'fit' into your environment. Monitor their speech, how they look and how they act to see if they fit your avatar.

■ As soon as possible force them to start talking about why they might want to work for you. Keep imagining them in your shop.

■ Never ask the normal, stupid 'tell me your strengths and weaknesses' question. You'll be faced with the usual line of people who tell you that they're perfectionists.

■ Do come up with this killer line: 'When I call your previous boss what will they say about you? What would they say are your good points and your bad points?' This line will get you a hell of a lot closer to the truth and for those folk who are telling great big lies you'll see it etched across their face.

Final key and absolutely vital point

Always have work to do between interviews. You'll need this because you WILL NOT be seeing all interviews through to the end of their time slot. You need to accept that some of the people who will sit in front of you are rubbish and that it was a mistake to get them in in the first place. Give them a polite couple of minutes and then pleasantly tell them that you have a lot of people to see and you'll get back to them. Be ruthless however difficult it may seem.

INDUCTION AND THE CONCEPT OF RULES

Now that we can assume you have put together a decent team, you need to help these people understand exactly what it is that you do and are trying to achieve within your business. Proper induction is nearly always completely overlooked by most coffee shops. The usual model involves last minute recruitment of unsuitable friends or family coupled with a ludicrous and, from a customer perspective, intensely irritating session of on the job 'we're all in this together isn't it fun' chaos.

General induction into your business is very different from pure coffee training. Coffee training is very specifically about ensuring that all coffee that leaves your business is of an exceptionally high standard. It's also quite different from any food training that you do. Depending on how much food preparation you are intending to do, your rules and induction for this can be quite lengthy. The basic sandwich rules within the taste section are an indication of the sorts of things that you need to cover in great depth during your food training.

Induction is about making sure that these new recruits fully understand, in intricate detail, exactly what your shiny new business is all about. For a new business this involves having at least one full day before you open when you go through exactly what they have to do, what you expect from them, and the standards and rules that you have in place within your business.

Johnny true story

I'm afraid I suffer(ed) badly from the illusion that I was such a great people person that I could change anyone. As such every time I made a bad recruitment decision I would work and coach the member of staff even when my partners were saying 'give up on him/her'. I would proudly then (in a few rare cases) point to a great employee who used to be terrible.

After two and a half years and countless disciplinary meetings in my office, I finally turned a young employee of ours into a loyal and hard working member of the team. Once more I pointed this out to my partners one of whom sat me down and went through the amount of time and effort that had gone into the process. He also reminded me how many other members of staff had been inconvenienced by her behavior and how many customers had been irritated whilst I was being the 'great mentor'.

He was, of course, absolutely right. So the lesson is, by all means work and coach poorly performing employees, but have a very strict cut off point and be very aware of the true cost of what you're doing.

INTRODUCING YOUR RULES

It's during induction that you need to introduce your rules. When we work through the formula we see that the passion has created the product with an exceptional taste and, hopefully, that has now been positioned correctly within the market. Later we'll develop the systems and marketing to help promote and control this, but you need to create a strong set of rules that surround your business. What these rules do is help to distill all the work that you've done up to this stage into a clear and easy to understand format that can be effectively drilled into a new starter's brain. These rules, a little like the concept of Bob and Brenda, need to become the cornerstone of your business and something that your new staff regard as second nature. They need to quote them back to you just as often as you quote them in your day-to-day management.

So what are these rules? Well, they're very different from your own personal rules that you established in the 'begin with the end in mind' section. Those rules govern how you behave within the business but your rules of operation need to govern how your employees work within the business. They are linked though. There will be aspects of your own rules and very strong elements of the passion that you originally developed to get you started within the rules.

If your original passion was based on outstanding coffee and a general and consistent frustration at the quality of the coffee, then this needs to become one of your rules. To be honest, any 'coffee' shop these days really has to have rules about coffee. But the point of these rules is not some glib statement like other coffee shops may come out with – they need to be backed up with your story and a strong sense of integrity, passion and authenticity. So if you proclaim that you will have the best coffee in the neighbourhood, then you really must have it. You have to live and breathe it and you can't allow Mervyn to arrive at the back door and let you cut a few corners. You'll lose all credibility with these rules if you allow them to be broken. That's the equivalent of that infuriating statement that teachers and parents use 'Do as I say, not as I do'. If you run your business like that then you're heading towards an expensive fall.

'No corner cutting' is a great rule that we have used personally and with clients. It's infuriating at times because we ALL want to cut corners but if you have laid out this rule and drummed it into everyone at induction (and in ongoing training) then you HAVE to stick to it – no matter how painful that may be in the short term. Not cutting corners is never painful in the long term because so few businesses adhere to standards like that.

Other rules can cover freshness, food quality, respect, customer service, cleanliness – anything relating to the business that really is hugely important to you and drove you to establish the business in the first place. To come up with your rules you need to get out a blank sheet of paper and list out all the things that really matter to you. Once you have this list you need to look at all the potential problems that you'll have within the business. This list, coupled with the 'passion' list, will help you to come up with a comprehensive list that encapsulates both of these.

This new long list now needs to be distilled down into a number of key points that will form the ultimate rules. Ideally you want no more than three because you'll find that people cannot consistently remember more than three without forcing themselves to remember, and that removes all the impetus from the process.

Once you have those three rules you can incorporate them into your induction (and all future training). But to get them to really stick you need to craft the story around how you came up with them. This story is what your staff will remember and it will also create a solid backbone to your business in terms of how they respect what you're trying to do. So regardless of how important you might feel 'making a huge amount of money' is, it's highly inadvisable to try to sell this as a rule to your staff. This is why the 'money men' who want to open coffee shops and chains will always struggle to create an environment that people want to work in (and by extension that customers want to purchase from). They cannot come up with rules that are authentic enough and ring true for employees. And never underestimate how many potential coffee shop employees actually see the job as a lifestyle option and will be put off by purely financial goals.

So your induction needs to be framed around these rules and must highlight and explain how they apply on a day-to-day basis. It needs to cover how staff should deal with customers, serve food, keep the store clean and also incredibly fine details like how the store should be left at the end of the night and include policies about, for example, opening in morning.

Johnny true story – My sandwich rules

In our sandwich bars my rules were very clear and ultimately these governed very strongly how the store looked and felt. They weren't properly balanced though and were too strongly biased towards the things that really mattered to me at that time. The three things that infuriated me in businesses of our type were:

1. Late deliveries – It always drove me up the walls that pizza delivery firms, taxis and many other businesses that delivered would seem to operate on a different time zone. 'It'll be there in 20 minutes' was always a huge lie it seemed to me.

2. Not having items on the menu. I hated visiting food establishments and making my mind up about something only to be told that they had 'run out'. When the second choice was missing too it's hard not to become really irritated with the business. Considering that most items in a sandwich bar are relatively generic and, if you do happen to encounter a huge rush, can be replenished at a local supermarket, there really is no excuse to have 'run out'.

3. Not opening on time. It's another pet hate but when you stand around outside any form of retail establishment waiting for them to open their doors five minutes after they are due to have opened something is a little wrong with the employee/customer respect ratio. To then, as is often the case, be greeted with nothing more than an 'I'm not a morning person' stare it's enough to drive pedantic idiots like me up the wall. With this in mind I operated a 'five minutes early' policy for our opening so that if someone was there on time they would be pleasantly surprised and not mildly irritated when they entered the store.

These three rules weren't the only things that mattered to me but they were three things that all staff knew I was really strong in enforcing. When I personally ran the first site we had, we didn't in a full 18 months ever have anything missing from the menu and nobody ever got a late delivery.

The rules collapsed a little when I left the day-to-day management of the business but that's because I hadn't fully grasped the concept of proper induction and systems yet. At that stage the business was strongly run in the 'you have to be there' fashion.

The problem was that these rules came out of things that irritated me but weren't properly thought through within the context of what would really appeal to customers. The end result was that the menu stayed a little staid because I was too busy worrying about keeping everything in stock and new items (which we were asked for) seemed like too much hassle.

These days I'd have very different rules to try and encompass a few other factors. Those rules would still ultimately exist but they could be wrapped up in a more general rule that might cover a few of them, i.e. we could say that our food must be exceptional, available and surprising. That would cover a number of issues in one rule – a method you should feel comfortable applying.

Changing rules

When Hugh and I started working together on consultancy projects, we were forced to change the rules for how we worked. Previously we have embarked together on some very loose alliances which were generally covered under the umbrella of us doing 'favours' for each other. When you do somebody a favour, clearly it's difficult to be bound by aggressive rules and clear standards of operation, so we worked out a set of rules that we could both agree to.

One of these rules was 'we do what we say'. This rule is a great rule for almost any business but it worked particularly well for us because it allowed us both to adhere to the rule and not hide behind a 'I'm doing you a favour' umbrella. Like any habit it took a little while to properly instill but now we both know that if we promise anything for each other it will be governed by the 'we do what we say' rule no matter how busy we may happen to be on our other projects. The secondary advantage of this is that you learn not to over-promise and commit to things that you won't be able to do. The embarrassment of not 'doing what we say' hangs over and ultimately makes you a little more realistic with deadlines and promises.

Be aware that this is a classic problem associated with working with friends and is even more prevalent in family businesses. The rules required to manage a business and work together are very different to those that we use socially and in families. If you are proposing to be in partnership with a friend then you need to take the time to sit down and map out these rules and expectations long before you ever switch on the coffee machine on day one.

Initially your induction should be done by the owner. In the early days there is nobody who is more capable of getting the passion and rules more articulately across to the new employees. The benefit of a decent induction is also that it helps you to weed out any 'goons' who have managed to slip through the interview process. As you grow and develop you should feel comfortable handing this over to your managers but make sure you still have a strong presence within the process. This can involve you dropping in for 20 minutes during the training or, when you get bigger, producing video of you highlighting your story and the reasons why you set up the business.

Another important aspect of induction training is that it needs to be something that the new employees participate in. Many (but clearly not all) coffee shop employees will be very uncomfortable within a classroom style situation so you need to try and avoid this. That means lots of hands on role play and interesting training that involves and tests them. We also find a field trip to a variety of local coffee shops extremely useful. Candidates need to come back with a report that highlights the good as well as the bad of rival operations. The temptation will be to impress you by only listing the bad things from rivals but this is the wrong way for them to think. They need to grasp how good some of the competition is and how hard it is to run all the minute detail of a coffee shop on a daily basis.

A final part of your induction should be to illustrate the economics of how a coffee shop works. To do this we start by asking employees how much they think an average coffee shop clears in profit out of every £1,000 in the till. The answers never really vary with the average employee assuming that a little under £500 goes to the bottom line. When you explain in detail (but in simplistic form) just how little money actually is net profit it makes your life infinitely easier in the future as you try to explain why it's important to control wastage and keep wage costs to a minimum.

POST-INDUCTION

Once you have your loyal little gang inducted/brain washed into your way of thinking, you need to keep following up. You need to make certain that this information isn't just part of a lovely day and evening where you tell them stories and get them to 'buy in' to your concept. It needs to be information that sticks with them and stays with them. These rules and your ethos need to become second nature to them.

To do this you must follow up. Any initial induction session must be followed up by either a formal process in about a month's time (with a test if you want) or by relentless repetition on your behalf (but only if you're working side by side with them on a regular basis).

Likewise, you need to make sure that you keep training and keep reinforcing long after the induction process is over. You MUST have regular training sessions and these rules must form the start, middle and end of each one, even if they're introduced subtly.

SOME FINAL RULES ABOUT TRAINING AND DEALING WITH YOUR STAFF

- **Pay them for training.** For goodness sake don't be mean and expect staff to spend time being trained without payment. This creates a very difficult dynamic from the start and you'll breed resentment and ultimately find it very difficult to get people to attend at all.

- **Make it fun.** You simply cannot preach from the front of the room like a geography teacher and expect people to become fully paid up ambassadors of your cause. Don't get over the top 'wacky' (because that is just irritating, but do make it fun).

- **Be passionate.** Again you cannot get them to buy in to your business unless you really show that you care about what you're trying to achieve. It's a big cliché (and we never seem to shut up about it) but if your business has no passion then you're ultimately resigned to mediocrity and probably a visit to the bankruptcy court.

- **Train regularly and in short bursts.** Aside from your initial induction training, you shouldn't hold sessions that last over an hour. To do this properly you need to have it well choreographed and keep it snappy. Get your points across with crystal clarity and move on. Every so often give them a few extra pounds to go out as a group afterwards and have a drink. Do NOT always attend these after training events yourself. It's important to keep some space between you and them.

- **Be careful how you behave at social functions.** It's extremely easy to mess up these events by having a couple of drinks too many or becoming too friendly with staff. Ultimately you need to remember that you're running a business and not a social club. This is a mistake far, far too many coffee shop owners make.

- **Hire slow – Fire fast.** This is one of those classic old clichés and it has taken both of us a while to fully grasp it but there is gold in those four words. If you make a mistake, rapidly deal with it. Neither of us believe the line that 'a leopard can't change its spots' but we both agree (as would most of our successful clients and colleagues) that less than 10% of employees or bad hires can be quickly turned around.

A sad little Johnny true story – Firing, the law and some harsh lessons

When we reached the heights of our third sandwich bar, I was 26 years of age and officially felt I was on my way to making my millions. At that level I kidded myself that we had a 'chain of sandwich bars' and my over-developed ego and confidence portrayed as this. I didn't walk, I strutted.

At this level I also adopted a more ruthless attitude towards firing staff. When you haven't worked side by side with people for a period of time it becomes much easier to get rid of them, particularly if they appear to be utterly unsuited to what you are trying to do.

In one of our sandwich bars we had a relatively young girl who was consistently creating problems. She was late nearly every day and clearly enjoyed quite a serious party habit. Regularly she would appear into work with 'love bites' on her neck and be very bleary after a late night. In a totally ad hoc fashion my manager of that unit used to tell her off and give her 'final warnings' but he was even younger and less experienced than me and obviously these warnings weren't properly recorded. On my morning 'ring round of our sites' (i.e three phone calls) I discovered that, yet again, this girl hadn't arrived into work. In a macho Alan Sugar fashion I told him to fire her. No ifs, no buts, she was out. Didn't she realise what an internationally famous business man I was about to become?

At about lunch time she arrived in. The manager relayed my tough stance and she was officially 'fired'. It felt good. I was no push over – that's for sure and people would think twice before messing with me in the future.

Two days later a letter came in from a local solicitor. He was representing our ex-employee who had been fired for arriving late after a hospital appointment to confirm she was pregnant. Not good. In indignation I then picked up the phone to him and ranted and raved about how bad her behaviour had been and how we hadn't the faintest idea that she was pregnant. He took detailed notes of my rant and somewhat dismissive attitude towards his poor pregnant client.

We spoke to our solicitor and he sat at his desk with his head in his hands. It was another one of those 'let me tell you boys a few facts about how you do business in the real world' conversations. To cut a long, painful and expensive story short we learnt a big lesson from this event. Over the course of the next 15 years I employed, in various forms, hundreds of people and we made a number of mistakes. We even ended up in court a few times for unfair dismissal claims but I never subsequently lost another case.

There are two key lessons.

1. Record everything. Legally you have obligations to record all disciplinary procedures and general official interaction with your employees but you need to take this a few stages further. Any 'chats' about anything that the employee isn't doing correctly must be filed away. This sounds very aggressive but the law is actually stacked against you and in most situations will lean towards the poor employee and against the big 'aggressive' employer. We can argue endlessly about the rights and wrongs of this but it won't do you any good. The only solution is to make sure you're extremely careful of what you say and record everything that you think may be relevant in the future. Notes can be as simple as a two-minute scribble (dated and timed) on a scrap of paper so don't think it involves endless hassle.

2. Use external agencies for advice. This book is not and never can be regarded as proper legal advice in terms of how to manage staff. The employment and retention of staff is a legal and ever shifting minefield and it makes absolutely no sense to try to stay 100% abreast of the law yourself. Please make sure you visit www.thecoffeeboys.com/legalstuff for further links and recommendations of people to use. I have always used external agencies to advise and create all our contracts and employee handbooks ever since that fateful 'you're fired' moment. Many of them aren't expensive and as far as I'm concerned any money that I've paid has been gained back many times.

The key issue with these agencies is to make sure that you stretch the edges of what they recommend though. They will be incredibly cautious and want you to make sure that all contact is in triplicate at every stage of the employee-contact phase. This will occasionally infuriate you but if you choose an option where they insure you against any problems then you have to do a fair amount of what they say. Ultimately what you are after is a balance of common sense, genuine and actual good employment practises and the 'i's dotted and 't's crossed should you end up in trouble or make a couple of rash decisions. What you must avoid is letting overtly pedantic legalities and red tape from letting you run your business in a pragmatic, flexible and reasonable fashion.

And here's one final thought about people and how you need to deal with them. It's a concept that can stick slightly in the throat of a few owners and managers because it stops allowing them to blame staff for the problems within their business:

There is generally no such thing as people problems – any problems that arise are part of a process or system that has gone wrong.

So what does that mean? What it means is that if you have a problem with an employee most of the time, it's your own fault. You have either recruited incorrectly or trained incorrectly. As such you need to do two things.

1. Fix the process or system that allowed this person to get into your business.

2. Fix or fire the employee (as quickly as possible).

Hugo true story – A world champion

While engaged on a consultancy project reviewing and fixing the operation of an extremely busy coffee bar that had lost its way, I came across a very interesting guy who was part time but with an obvious 'Je ne sais quois'. He was enthusiastic, bright, had a great attitude and I asked him to help me lead the barista team, few of whom even knew what a barista was. We got to work and made a difference over the next few months doubling turnover and ending up with a great product offer leaving a refit as the final part of the jigsaw.

I completed the job and the part timer was asked to do some training. From there he began roasting and learning and learning and learning. He subsequently won the World Barista Championship and developed into one of the coffee world's great experts with a real passion for what he does. Talent is all around us but you must keep looking for it and help to encourage and nurture it. It's a full-time job in itself but ultimately can be extremely rewarding for all concerned.

5 Marketing

Marketing includes PR (and word of mouth), direct marketing, advertising, merchandising and stealing ideas from other businesses and industries.

Marketing is ultimately really about making people want to buy. As such before we launch into any tips techniques or strategies, it's important to grasp what this means at a really fundamental level. It's time for . . . a key concept!

A Johnny key concept – Desire and trust

Every week we get emails from people saying how completely frustrated they are about their businesses. They say they are doing everything right and that they just cannot understand why they aren't busier. They complain that the particular competitor they have down the road seems to be far busier and yet, in their eyes, doesn't do as good a job.

It is frustrating but the fact is that the difference between a profitable business and a non-profitable business is generally the result of nothing to do with location or a bad business plan or some of those other factors that we might read about in a book. The difference is that the successful guys have managed to master two key skills.

Those skills are the ability to create desire and trust. That's it.

We all have various daft things that we spend money on – almost regardless of whether we can afford it or not. In Western society nearly all our purchasing decisions are driven by emotion and therefore there is always a choice. We choose to buy one thing over another for all sorts of reasons, most of which bear no relation to why we say we buy them. We buy certain types of wine, shoes, golf clubs, chocolate, magazines, newspapers, clothes, cars, computers – all based on a priority that we have in our mind. And most of the time these priorities are driven by desire and trust.

Ask an Apple Mac user to go back to a PC and he'll smirk in an infuriatingly smug way – it'll never happen. The Apple Ipod is clearly not the best MP3 player but the desirability quotient is through the roof. You can buy a comparable PC for about a third of the price of a Mac and that doesn't make the slightest difference. Apple has huge trust built up with their customers too. Just walk into your local Apple store to see both concepts in action. Desire is clearly there and it exhibits a lifestyle that we all aspire to, but also they have cleverly crafted all manner of inexpensive ways to help you out with your Apple products. You know that if something goes wrong there is an aspirational geek just waiting to answer your questions in a pleasant and highly trained manner. So your trust that 'everything will be all right' is huge and coupled with the desirability quotient it's almost a wonder that we don't all use Macs.

We don't for a variety of reasons though. Some of us actually rebel against that kind of thing and can become mildly irritated by the smugness of it. That's okay though – desire and trust will be very different for different people and as ever you shouldn't try and be all things to everybody.

Desire and trust has nothing to do with income or socio-economic status. As an experiment, drive through the worst housing estate in your local area and look at the walls of the houses. You'll see that nearly every house has a satellite dish on the wall, and peer through the window to see the big TV. I didn't get satellite until last year and only then because it was part of the SKY broadband deal.

I first grasped this concept about 15 years ago when I was operating my first couple of sandwich bars. Myself and my business partner were the only people in our business who didn't have satellite. We were the ones earning the 'big bucks' and most of our staff were earning £3 or £4 per hour (this was pre-minimum wage days). But what mattered to them was having satellite TV and yet I felt I couldn't afford or justify it. So this has nothing to do with the class system or even some sense of snobbery – it's all to do with desire and human nature driving us to buy certain things or not.

There is a notion that perhaps we might have all 'wised up' as a result of the credit crunch but again that is farcical. The credit crunch is almost the perfect example of why this actually is the truth. It involved people spending far too much money on things that they wanted (or desired) even though they couldn't afford it. That's human nature. Certainly there are a few obstacles in the way now in terms of relentlessly buying the big things, but for small luxuries like a coffee? There still has to be and clearly is plenty of money for that. The proof lies in those clients of mine who are utterly unaffected by the recession – but these folk are doing a shockingly good job.

So if selling IS really all about desire and trust which is the most important? Trust is vital but actually in certain situations it's not even essential. We have all backed off from various purchasing decisions, even if we felt we really wanted them, just because we didn't quite trust whoever was selling to us and again that comes right down to the level of food and drink. Sometimes you read a menu and it's organic this or local that and you find a couple of little flaws that don't add up. You see a frozen food delivery van at the back door or find 'local asparagus' in October. If the desire that has been created isn't strong enough then you simply won't return. You'll feel ripped off and that's the relationship over.

But . . . if you can crank the desire up to such a level that it starts to blot out even the lack of trust then you have a sure-fire winner. Take the example of the people who allow themselves to get scammed by those Nigerian emails. Or even those terribly lonely people who get scammed by potential wives or husbands on the internet. Deep down we all know when something is too good to be true or when we're being scammed, but the desire for that £200,000 from Nigeria or the perfect relationship can help to blot that out. It's easy to think 'Oh I'm much cleverer than that', or 'my customers aren't like that' but that simply isn't the case. We're all driven by the same basic needs. Of course 'WE' wouldn't get caught up by a scammer, but we still make our purchasing decisions every day in life based on desire. Desire is the ROOT of all sales and you should never forget that.

Your job, in a new or existing coffee shop, is to up the ante in terms of desire and trust. You have to create a product so delicious in an environment that is so wonderful that you become the equivalent of an Apple Store. At that level you can sell almost anything and for almost any price. That is the very essence of making people buy and no clever marketing tactics or strategies can ever compensate for a product that isn't desired or a business that customers don't trust.

CREATING DESIRE

So marketing starts with the creation of desire. In any project we always start with the understanding that everything begins with quality. In many sites and with the right product you can actually manage to avoid all traditional marketing if your quality is of such an epic level (and a true epic level – not your own imagined levels) that people will simply tell each other about your wonderful business.

But that isn't always easy to achieve. And if you can't quite produce food and coffee that is so good that your customers are driven to endlessly talk about you, then you need to dig a little deeper into the marketing bag of tricks. Marketing is at heart pure psychology. It's about understanding at a remarkably deep level (if you can) just what it is that makes people tick and why they behave in certain ways. Ultimately the behaviour that we're most interested in is why they will pay for a product. If you can fully tap into why people buy then the world is your oyster (or little chocolate muffin at the very least).

But before we go into specifics we wanted to go through a basic concept that lies at the very heart of why people might decide to visit your shop as a result of a marketing effort.

HOW TO DRIVE LOADS OF CUSTOMERS INTO YOUR SHOP

Legendary copywriter Roy H Williams talks about the world's best traffic builder in his seminal book *The Wizard of Ads*. He talks about how the best solution to drive people into your store is simply to dress three employees up as policemen and get them to direct people into your shop. When it is full they take off their uniforms and come in and try to sell them stuff. Sounds great in principle – you'd have a shop full of people but would they actually be likely customers for your product?

The point behind this is that it is about as effective as most general advertising and it is almost exactly what most coffee shop operators do in an effort to try and get new business. They simply put an ad in the paper and try to 'drive traffic' to their store. Most of the time this ad has been created by the local paper and reveals little more than the name and address of their business and perhaps a few snippets from the menu.

Advertising in particular and marketing in general are just about the most misunderstood parts of running a business and yet they are, almost without exception, something that people seem to think they know something about. If you were to invite ten of your friends to help you with the new advert or flyer that you're going to use to set up your business the chances are that pretty much all of them would be keen to offer an opinion. If you were to ask those same ten people to help you choose a new till system or a accounting package, the chances are that they would all say they weren't qualified to do so.

People think that because they've watched or read advertising their entire lives that they can offer sound judgement and assistance to do so. The reality is that they are equally as well placed to offer advice on your accounting package as they are on your marketing efforts. And, unless you have actually studied marketing properly, you're likely to be in exactly the same situation.

Johnny true story – The long saga of the 90-year-old advertising book

My degree was actually in business and marketing, and in the following year after I left university I took my professional marketing exams. As a consequence of this, when I started my first business I felt that the one thing I was properly capable of doing was producing great marketing. I thought that, because of the impressive letters after my name, I was going to produce great marketing that would force the business forward in an exciting way.

The reality couldn't be further from the truth. If I'm honest in our first business we got lucky. We produced the right product for the right time and simply worked like mad men in an endearingly scatter brained manner (as only business people in their twenties can do) to grow what ended up being a remarkably large business.

Along the way I produced some vaguely interesting pieces of marketing but in essence it had very little to do with my abilities and education and everything to do with having a great product at the right time.

When I started my next business things were very different. We had no money and were operating in a fearsomely competitive market – fish and chips. They are the ultimate 'me-too' product in the sense that most shops sell almost exactly the same thing and therefore it is very difficult to differentiate in any other way than by price. And simply selling a product cheaper than the competition is a great way to work both yourself and the competition into an early grave.

So this is when I really learnt about marketing. During this phase I read dozens of classic books on both advertising and marketing. The full list of these books is available at www.freecoffeeboys.com, but there was one book that really stood out and opened my eyes to the correct way to sell food and drink.

It was an amazing book by an old advertising guru called Claude Hopkins. The book was called *Scientific Advertising* and in it Hopkins elaborated on his theories of 'Reason Why' marketing, and how all advertising and marketing should exist only to sell something and that it should always be measurable. This resonated very closely with me since I had become a victim of the advertising world's version of 'Mervyn the Salesman'. Advertising Mervyn seeks to sell you, in an increasingly desperate fashion, space in his newspaper or magazine at a 'special price'. When you start to query exactly what you might be getting out of your advertising, Mervyn will insist that 'advertising doesn't work like that'. He will try to persuade you that people need to see your advert up to a dozen times before they take action and that it is a 'drip drip' effect.

The reality of 'Mervyn' in an advertising environment is that Mervyn knows the square root of nothing about advertising. Mervyn is a salesman and he knows about selling. He knows that if he feeds you the same old lines about repetition that he is likely to secure repeat business from you and if you stop after the fourth or fifth week because you've had no success then it's your own stupid fault because you simply haven't allowed the customers to see the advert enough.

Here are the facts: If your advert doesn't work first time . . . it's a bad advert, or it's in the wrong publication. It's that simple and you must ALWAYS make sure you can actually quantify what those results are.

One story in the Claude Hopkins book fascinated me and inspired me with an idea. Claude had been appointed by Schlitz Beer to improve their sales. They were sitting at number nine in sales and wanted to get to number one – an admirable goal certainly, but clearly not an easy challenge. Hopkins started to dig deep into their business to find out exactly what they did. He was really passionate about finding out real facts behind a product and about doing his research.

He discovered that most beer advertising involved the word 'pure' but this really meant nothing. It was just, in his words, a 'platitude'. When he dug deep into how Schlitz beer was produced he discovered some incredible facts. The bottles were washed four times by machinery, the water for the beer came from 4,000 feet below the ground, 1,018 experiments had been made to attain a yeast that gave the correct flavour for the beer, and all the yeast for Schlitz beer was forever made from that adopted mother cell.

These facts are something that the consumer simply didn't know and generally would be fascinated to discover. The problem, said Schlitz, was that all beer was made that way – what they were doing wasn't unique. But Hopkins persevered and wrote extensive 'long copy' (i.e. lots of text) adverts where he explained this process. He pictured the plate glass where the beer was filtered in filtered air and the white wood pulp through which every drop was cleared. In short he told the story, in intricate detail, of how they made their beer.

The result of these adverts? . . .

Schlitz went to number one and stayed there for 20 years.

I loved this story. It seemed to make huge sense to me and seemed to be far more relevant to the marketing of food and drink than almost every advert I had produced or seen other operators produce. So with that in mind I started an experiment. I took five products that we were selling and told their 'story' in an advert in the local paper. These were old fashioned 'long copy' adverts with an accompanying photo of the product and a limited time Buy One Get One Free (BOGOF) offer on the product in question. The local advertising guy in our paper looked at me as if I had two heads when I showed him what I was proposing to do. Bear in mind, these adverts were simply produced and set by me in Microsoft Word and I am about as close to being a graphic designer as Hugh is to running a four-minute mile.

Since I was offering him money however, he obviously was happy to print the ads. In his words though they would be a 'disaster'. He felt that nobody would ever bother to read all those facts about each product and that they were boring.

The result?

Like Hopkins's ads it totally transformed our business. The business was jammed for those ten weeks that we ran the ad. But the real proof is always what happens after you finish a promotion. How many of these people would stay as loyal customers?

In our case, after the initial lift during the ad campaign, our sales increased by 25%. This produced about a 75% increase in our bottom line profit. It also dramatically increased the value of the business which we then sold at a premium a few months later.

So marketing ultimately is, at its most simplistic, about creating a product that is so good that it sells itself. That's a tough call, so the essence of marketing beyond that, is to make sure that you tell a story about your products that is enormously compelling to the customers.

That story doesn't have to be reproduced in a newspaper advert. It can be part of a leaflet drop or contained in product information sheets placed within the shop. It must always be on the tip of your staff's tongue. Your induction program needs to labour heavily on the stories behind your products and the huge lengths that you go to to make them great.

6 Systems

Systems are one of those tedious aspects of running a business that most owners and prospective owners like to ignore, but they really are THE fundamental key to creating the dream business you originally envisioned. As we've discussed in the 'Start with the end in mind' section, you really need to have a grasp of what it is that you want out of this new business and, regardless of what it is you need really good systems to achieve that goal.

> Most entrepreneurs are merely technicians with an entrepreneurial seizure. Most entrepreneurs fail because you are working IN your business rather than ON your business.
>
> Michael Gerber

LOOKING AT THREE SCENARIOS

Let's assume three scenarios.

1. The owner operator – let's call her Jill

Jill sees her new coffee shop as part of a wonderful new lifestyle. She doesn't want more than one site as she intends to be there every day. She has read the entrepreneurial biographies and is all set to do 'whatever it takes'. She's 'not afraid of hard work' and is prepared to be 'up until three in the morning to get things going'. Jill is full of adrenalin and bravado to get it going but feels confident that the end goal will be worth it. She expects that about six months of hard graft will be all that's necessary to get a good team around her 'licked into shape' and then she can start to enjoy it a bit and have a few days off.

She also hopes that this new lifestyle will also earn her a bit of extra money. She's not really even doing it for the money (it's more of a lifestyle decision) but feels confident that owning her own business is bound to be more profitable than her normal job. The big advantage is that she'll be able to toddle in late every so often and get off early to see a few of those school plays she missed when she was working for 'the man'.

Her overall intention is NOT world domination through her coffee shop and she hopes to be still involved on a day-to-day basis with the business. She intends to be actually working 'in' the business at least four or five days a week. It's an admirable goal. It sounds lovely and indeed can even work for some people.

But what happens if she falls sick? What happens when she goes on holiday? What happens during the two or three hours when Jill decides to come in late or go home early?

Jill simply expects to have lots of 'great people' around her who by this stage will know what to do. But will they fully understand her vision and make sure it works as seamlessly as she does? And what will happen if they happen to be on holiday or fall ill at the same time as Jill needs time off? Or what happens if she perhaps can't find people who buy into her concept just as strongly as she does?

2. The 'business man' – let's call him Derek

Derek has made a little bit of money in other businesses. He has a nice suit and possibly a BMW or Mercedes. Derek sees the coffee shop business as a much more attractive alternative to what he normally does. He sits at home one night and works out a few figures. He works out the margin on coffee and sits back in his chair in awe. He immediately jumps to the conclusion that there are vast fortunes to be made in the coffee business.

So Derek decides to open a coffee shop. He looks at the costs and again is excited at what he sees. There aren't hugely expensive equipment costs and it seems to be a heck of a lot cheaper to put together than a restaurant. He'll create a decent product and then just 'put in a good manager' and away he'll go. If it all goes well he may open a second one but to begin with it seems as if this is the easiest business he's ever been involved with and at those margins how could you possibly go wrong?

But Derek's other businesses are a little simpler. They generally don't change on an hourly basis. They generally don't deal with hundreds of different customers every day. They don't require complete re-stocking every few days and they certainly don't have to deal with such frequent product variability. They don't deal with so much cash. They don't have such a transient workforce. They don't have employees who laugh at their jobs and assume that they will never have a career in that industry.

Derek has a few surprises waiting for him.

3. The entrepreneur – let's call him Hector (for that is indeed a great name)

Hector has a vision and a dream. Hector sees a huge empire ahead of him. He sees dozens of 'Hector's coffee houses' out there serving the best coffee in the land and the best chocolate brownie in the known universe. He has a great plan and has raised a fair bit of money due to his charm and charisma.

Hector hopes to get two shops open in the first year and then start opening at a rate of several a year for the next five to ten years and then sell out for the big bucks – yehaa!

Hector has been a barista for a few years and is highly skilled in his art. It's arguable that Hector possibly could create the best espresso in the city. In Hector's mind as long as he has great coffee in a funky environment all the rest will just happen. I mean how hard can the rest be? How hard can it be to manage all those other areas of the business? The real skill is in the 'art' of espresso.

Underestimating the importance of systems

These are all clichés for sure. But they all represent the sort of potential owners and existing operators that we see on an extremely regular basis. They don't, by any means, encapsulate all the potential owners of coffee shops but they do all share a very similar problem. All of them will radically underestimate the importance of systems in all parts of the business.

Jill

Jill's character is extremely common and indeed one of the saddest of all. Jill is unlikely to have a lot of spare cash and will almost certainly underestimate how much money she needs to get the business into profit. But most importantly of all, Jill will fall prey to the biggest myth in business: 'You have to be there.'

She will quickly discover that she has actually got little or no skills in recruitment, training and managing, so, with her vision strong in her mind, she will decide to be there every hour that her shop is open and to just bully the whole operation into some form of a profitable business. She will either try to do everything herself for fear of others doing it the wrong way or she'll rant and rave in pressurised situations and create a deeply unpleasant situation for everyone. Deeply unpleasant situations are rarely a great place to work, so she'll quickly lose any decent staff she might have had and will continually moan that 'you just can't get the staff' or 'nobody wants to work hard these days'.

She will quickly become exhausted and realise that all she has done is create a trap for herself and the few snatched moments at her daughter's school play that she finally makes it to are enveloped in a sense of panic whilst she wonders exactly what sort of mess is being created back at her business. The problem becomes more acute if she actually does manage to make a bit of money. The reality is that a number of 'Jills' do make a little money because they have a tendency to quite often produce great food. It may take them 12 hours a day, six days a week, to do so, but at the end of the year they will show a profit, albeit at a rate that works out at less than minimum wage.

The reason why this is a problem is that it almost shows some vindication for her working style. She may even, after a couple of years, see herself as a business woman and join some local business organisations. There she will meet a mixture of other Jills and a few men in shiny suits who will try to sell her insurance. The Jills (either male or female) will all huddle together in a support group avoiding the shiny suited insurance reps and consoling themselves that indeed 'you DO have to be there'. They agree that it's tough but go back home feeling that this is just the way it has to be.

Jill is wrong. Terribly, tragically wrong. Jill will work herself into an early grave. And the worst thing of all? The industry is full to the brim with Jills.

Derek

Derek isn't so tragic but he still won't have a great time. The advantage of Derek's scenario is that it won't be as prolonged as Jill's. He'll get in there, lose a fair bit of money, downscale a few of his retirement plans, and quickly revert back to what he was doing before. He will, older and wiser, lie on the beach at Blackpool and think 'crikey that was a lucky escape – there really is no way you can make money in that business'.

The problem is that Derek will simply fail to grasp that the systems required to operate and run a great coffee shop require a delicate mix of passion, logic and great people skills. It is a long way from the skills that are required to set up and supervise a production line. Derek will cut corners and cut costs and view it in a clinical business fashion which is totally counterproductive to a business like the coffee shop business. He will singularly fail to recognise that he needs to get his staff to really buy into the vision of what it is that he is trying to do. The problem is that the vision of what he is trying to do is impossible for anyone other than his bank manager to buy into. Derek just wants to make a lot of money and that will immediately become transparent to both his customers and staff.

He will have isolated moments where it appears to go okay, perhaps when he chances upon a decent manager, but his inability to make them feel part of something great will gradually drive them away to greener pastures. Very soon Derek will be back to a chaotic square one.

Derek will try to over compensate for not being busy enough and raise his prices. And gradually his business will totally fail.

Hector

Hector has a chance but he has a lot of lessons to learn. Hector grasps the emotional side of the business and will have a fairly relentless desire to produce great coffee and food. Hector is likely to do okay for the first while. He'll go through the classic mistakes of not focusing on his margin and wage costs and learn quite quickly that he isn't making any money, but in general he's a bright boy and should fairly rapidly come up with a superficially quite good business. His passion for great coffee will bleed over into his food offering and he will either source decent suppliers or work hard late into the night developing his own products. One way or another though he will end up with a decent offer.

Likewise his passion and quality will make it fairly easy for him to recruit some decent staff. Hector is young and single and will enjoy the buzz of working with young, passionate staff. He'll pull together a decent team and they'll all work hard to create a fun place to both work in and buy coffee from. But he'll start to make mistakes. He'll socialise with staff and expect them to telepathically know what he wants done. Because they are now his friends he will struggle to play the 'big boss' and they will joke a little bit too much with him in front of customers and more junior staff.

When he is away for a few days, standards will slip again. The employees will not see that standards need to be kept relentlessly high and will just like working in a cool place. They will become the kinds of cool baristas who regard themselves as being above the customer.

So with standards slipping slightly but everything still superficially okay Hector will open his second site and put his best 'friend' in charge of the old place. He will work like a mad man building this new empire and just about cope. And then he'll meet with his accountant. This won't be a nice meeting because he'll quickly realise that he's not making any more money than he was in the early days of the first site. He'll also rant and rave a bit and begin a few sleepness nights. His house in on the line. He's working 12-hour days and he simply cannot control all the staff properly and ensure all the food and coffee is perfect. But he'll keep at it.

Gradually he'll put some systems and checks in place. He'll produce opening and closing checklists and start to do yearly appraisals for his staff. He'll produce job descriptions and a basic training program for new starts. Slowly things will get a little better and then he'll see a third site . . .

In the third site he again works very hard but there are problems. He really is struggling with the new staff here and they don't really 'get' his business in the same way that his staff did in the first site. The first site staff are complaining that they never see him and all thoughts of finding the time for yearly appraisals has gone totally out the window. Again he meets with his accountant and again it's a bit of a shock.

The great dream of Hector's Coffee House has turned into a nightmare.

Hector works huge hours and spends all day every day fire-fighting. Standards are highly variable in each of his outlets and entirely dependent on the staff working on that particular day.

So why the long-winded stories?

Well these stories are simple distillations of the people we see all the time. They are distillations of actual businesses that we know and indeed, in a couple of cases, have actually operated ourselves as we climbed the slippery slope of understanding this industry.

The point is all three scenarios produce a nightmare. Jill and Hector just about manage to hang on and Derek goes out of business. Your job is to do your very best to avoid the chance that you might be either Derek, Hector or Jill. And what is the solution?

The solution is systems and processes.

Edward Deming – the man who was credited with taking Japan out of the mess it was in immediately after the second world war was quoted as saying:

If you can't describe what you are doing as a process, you do not know what you are doing.

This is a very hard lesson to learn for many coffee shop operators but that's really what a coffee shop is (or indeed should be). It needs to be a system of processes that seamlessly govern everything that you do. Deming helped to transform Japan into an economic superpower, and you need to do the same thing with your new business.

Don't forget this is all part of a formula though. A proven formula that we have put in place within our own businesses and with other clients. And that means that it still starts with passion.

But the passion for superb food and coffee must very quickly be wrapped up into a clean and coherent system that allows you to create a business and not just a job that you bought yourself.

If you don't create these systems and look at every stage as a process then you will end up working huge hours and letting life pass you by. Here are some startling facts:

- The average US entrepreneur works 14 weeks more per year than they did in 1969.

- The average working person spends twice as much time dealing with emails as they do with their children.

That is a truly frightening statistic but it's one that you really need to grasp and be aware off. These days coffee shops are often open seven days a week and several evenings. We live in a 24-hour society and your new business can take advantage of that. But unless you properly grasp at the outset that you are NOT going to be there all that time, and, more importantly, that it will operate just as well when you aren't there, then you need to place this book to one side and go back into work tomorrow and give your boss a big hug. Sit him or her down and tell them that you want to forget all that nonsense about you leaving.

From day one your goal needs to be to create systems around every problem that arises. A system and a process so powerful that the problem doesn't arise again. That is your job. That is how you will drive the business and how you will create this dream life. This is a spectacularly difficult thing for many start up entrepreneurs to grasp. They see the initial phase as being all about putting these fires out and individually solving problems. That, they presume, is their role and generally it's something that they do best. When the problem is sorted they tell everyone not to make the mistake again and expect that it won't happen. When it does they're shocked and mutter to themselves 'but I told them, how could they be so stupid!'

Let's take a real life scenario to help illustrate the point.

REAL LIFE SCENARIO: BOB SETS UP A COFFEE BAR

It's a relatively classic speciality coffee bar style with the emphasis on coffee and buns and the lunchtime food offering being secondary. He has a range of panini and sandwiches that are sold at lunch and about half of them are sold to order, i.e. made up from scratch. Bob has tried a variety of other solutions (including bought in panini) and feels that this method gives his customers the best taste. He has patiently stood in his coffee bar with his partner late one night and made up all the paninis individually with a stop watch. The time taken for each one varies between 40 seconds and 55 seconds before they are put on the panini grill. He feels that this extra time, over that which will be used to open a package bought from another supplier, is well worth taking and helps differentiate him from his local competitors.

It's all sound logic. Bob is indeed probably correct.

The problem is that in the real world this isn't working. The panini are taking a lot longer to make. His staff are 'faffing about' and taking up to five minutes to get a single panini ready. Nobody is getting close to the 40-second goal and it is really starting to disrupt his lunchtime service. Worse still, there are a number of mistakes being made and he is running out of crucial ingredients and having to make substitutions.

His local market is generally office workers and they have limited time. It doesn't matter that Bob's panini is ultimately better than the competition. If there's a queue that takes 20 minutes to get to the end of then that simply won't work for them – they'll go elsewhere and indeed that is what is happening. Bob has spoken to a number of his morning customers who don't bother with him for lunch for that very reason.

So Bob highlights a couple of his slowest workers and goes through the whole process with them again in an exasperated fashion. They improve a little but others are still slow and there seems to be huge mess created with this increased speed. Bob gets cross and starts the classic owner operator rant 'You just can't get the staff!'

What Bob needs to realise is that there are several processes in operation here. One is the physical process and surroundings with which they administer the order. Another is the way that the ingredients for the orders are produced and then stored. And another is the method with which he actually trains his staff. There may be more but at this stage let's just deal with those three. Bob needs to sit down quietly with his big pad of A3 paper and work out exactly what is going on. He needs to do this after close of business and without distractions. He also needs at least one intelligent and rational member of staff with him who can honestly tell him the problems.

1. The ordering and production process

This process starts with the order from the till which is generally shouted across to the person in charge of making the panini. Sometimes customers want slightly different variations in their panini and this causes problems. These variations all have to be held in the production person's mind since there is no system for recording it. A number of the products are held in different fridges and there is no set place for them on a day-to-day basis. Sometimes it can take three of four attempts to find where the chicken is or the tomatoes are.

Bob maps out the process in detail and looks at each stage. He decides that one of the biggest blocks in the process is the actual order production so puts down as an action point that he needs to look into a new till system that can produce a food order ticket. He calculates that his wastage with incorrect orders is about £50 per month and that doesn't even cover the hidden cost of the disgruntled customers, so he feels he can afford to spend a little in this area.

He also clearly sees that the process is slow because there is no clear system for storing all the prepared products. So he buys a new sandwich prep station which has a row of refrigerated containers at the back and a decent food service counter at the front. All shelves within the fridge are then mapped out in terms of both food hygiene regulations and also speed of access. This map is laminated and placed on the inside of the fridge. All staff are trained in the new system.

Bob and his assistant set up a new work station and make certain that everything is in place and to hand. He adopts the classic restaurant technique of getting 'mise en place' before service. What this means is that everything is properly placed and to hand. This leads him to address the second issue.

2. Preparation

Bob notes that all the preparation is done in an incoherent fashion. People are randomly allocated jobs to do and fit them in and around other tasks. Different people cut things in different ways and in different sizes. There are irregular amounts of prepared ingredients each day which sometimes means that extra items need to be prepped during the lunchtime service which slows everything down.

He breaks the preparation down into specific areas and times exactly how long it should take for each task. He creates rules as to the sizings of items and takes pictures of perfectly 'prepped' food. He establishes new hygiene regulations to ensure that not only is the food properly produced, but that it is stored at the correct temperatures and in the correct areas. He establishes minimum preparation quantities for each day and produces a weekly chart to show how this fluctuates with the changing demands during the week.

Finally, he establishes systems for identifying who is capable of producing the food the fastest and looks into making sure that all his staff can more effectively operate at the same level. Which leads him on to the next stage.

3. Recruitment and training of staff

Bob quickly realises that he has been 'selling a dream' to potential employees in an effort to recruit them. He has been painting a picture of an idyllic job where the employees simply make coffee and have great fun in a buzzing, exciting environment.

He has conveniently ignored the harsh realities of food preparation, very busy times, cleaning, and some of the other essential parts of working in any coffee shop. This has created resentment with his staff and this has lead to them, whether consciously or not, operating in a slow and resistant way when they are producing paninis.

Also they are trained in an entirely ad hoc way in terms of making paninis. He shows some staff how to make a few of them and then hands it over to them to show the rest. Sometimes a new member of staff can be shown how to make a panini by a member of staff who was only shown herself less than a week previously. This results in serious inconsistency and a lack of control over both the gross profit margin and the quality of the product.

Bob goes back to basics. He completely redesigns his recruitment policy and the interview process. He makes sure that all potential staff completely understand what is expected of them long before they ever start and he radically changes how they are trained. He maps out every stage of the process and ensures that every panini that is produced is only created by someone who has been properly trained. He takes pictures of each of the perfect final paninis and records a short video on his camcorder to show all new staff so that he can get his message across without having to be there. He appoints one member of staff to deal with the training and spends extensive time with her initially to ensure that she grasps the importance of this part of the business.

Outcome of having processes in place

The result is that within a relatively short period of time Bob has transformed both the quality and the profit that he earns from his paninis. He needs to do a little bit of marketing to help improve sales and pull back those customers that he lost, but very quickly the business is at a new level. Best of all he is able to devote more of his time to physically managing and developing the business, rather than getting stressed and dealing with the fall-out of the badly made paninis.

The point behind this story is to help illustrate that generally any issue that you come across will have a lot of factors affecting it – all of which are a process and all of which need a system to control. Many operators simply will not accept this. They carry on putting sticking plasters on problems and fighting fires daily and assume that that is simply the way it has to be.

If you can start up your business with this attitude and mindset you'll find yourself way ahead of the pack within six months. Remember the mantra:

> ### There are no such things as people problems – there are only system problems.

If you can keep that in your mind every time you become exasperated over an issue then you'll make life a LOT easier.

This, of course, will be easier said than done. The numerous reality restaurant shows on either side of the Atlantic prove just how much operators and potential operators underestimate just how much work will be required to properly operate their business. The 'dream' is almost instantly shattered and it makes fantastic television to see the huge meltdowns and temper tantrums that evolve from this. You need to be acutely aware of this since we see it on a consistent basis within our consultancy business too.

The problem is that you're going to be immediately projected into a world of new problems and the automatic thing to do will be to just fix it and then carry on the next day in the same vein. This will become your habit and your employees will quickly accept this as the way. You MUST start day one with the understanding that you are not the short-term fixer and you will not always be at the end of the phone for every little problem.

Let's look at a few potential and somewhat petty problems that will arise and how you need to deal with them.

SUPPLIER CONTACT DETAILS

Initially these will all be held in your diary or mobile phone. You will have spent the previous few months building up these contacts and creating rapport with suppliers to ensure the launch and first week or so go as smoothly as possible. But very quickly problems will happen when you're not there. Perhaps the water boiler will break down and you are the guy who normally fixes it or phones the electrician. But you're not there – you're at your daughter's school play. The shop phones you and, to your acute embarrassment, you leave the hall to take the call. It takes ten minutes to deal with it and by this time you've missed your daughter's 'bit' in the play. She's not happy and you descend into parental guilt hell – always a bad place to be.

The reality is that these situations rarely happen in such emotive circumstances but they do happen all the time in less extreme ways. The frankly ludicrous calls that we hear, on an almost daily basis, from clients regarding their shops (and in many cases multi-site stores) show that these are issues that exist at EVERY level and even with experienced operators.

The key here is to ensure that all of the relevant details are properly produced on a clean sheet of laminated paper. All suppliers, complete with names and mobile numbers, need to be on this sheet. Specific items of equipment need to have extra details on them. You don't want expensive engineer call outs if all that is needed is a new fuse.

So in this situation you sort the problem by phone and then go back home that night and create the system to ensure it doesn't happen again.

DELIVERY PROBLEMS

You WILL have delivery problems and you need to be aware of this from the very beginning. Driver theft is a big issue, as well as classic and simpler problems. Let's assume your driver is short of a couple of items but the delivery note and invoice shows that they have been delivered. He says to your member of staff not to worry about it and that he'll deliver it next time. This happens every single day throughout the country and it is not good enough. Whether he is honest or not, these things can very quickly be forgotten and you won't know anything about it. You may find a scribbled note on the delivery docket, but most of the time these are illegible and will mean nothing when you (or your bookkeeper) do your invoices at the end of the month.

The key is to create a goods-in system, just like you were a large business. It will annoy a few suppliers since it may slow down deliveries a fraction, and for small suppliers it removes an element of friendly trust, but it is essential. Everything must be counted or weighed when it comes in and it must be marked off in a delivery book or sheet. Any problems or issues relating to the delivery must be clearly marked on this sheet as well as the delivery docket. If a further delivery comes in to make up for the mistake then this must be marked too.

ALL staff must be aware of this system and trained in how it operates. It makes it vastly harder for a driver to steal. A little like the burglar who moves along from house to house to find one without an obvious burglar alarm, the dodgy driver will simply avoid stealing from your order and move on to the next site. Likewise the accounts staff at the suppliers will soon learn that you are very fussy with your deliveries and make sure that any issues are corrected beforehand.

INGREDIENT PROBLEMS

When setting up your initial food and drink offer you will hopefully allow your passion to run strong. You will ensure that you have the best ham you can find for your sandwiches and choose a milk supplier who fully understands the unique requirements of milk for coffee bars operating 12 months of the year. You will stay resolute when Mervyn The Salesman arrives at the back door with a few 'the customer will never know' products.

But what happens when you aren't there? A slightly peculiar thing evolves in nearly all businesses of this type – the staff seem to think they're doing you a favour by cutting costs. The odd thing is they rarely pay any attention to cutting costs on things like electricity bills or general wastage but they will be delighted to shave a few pennies here and there with ingredient costs. As we've discussed before your initial passion is tough enough to get through to them but over time you'll find it even harder to keep at the forefront of your mind.

What this does is produce scenarios whereby staff will believe 'Mervyn' or even decide that the bargains at your local supermarket are better for the customer than what you normally buy. Very quickly, unless you are careful, you'll find all sorts of 'great bargains' being reproduced for sale in your lovely new coffee bar. You'll find all manner of nonsense suddenly surrounding the till because 'a customer asked for it'.

This is why you need really, really clear product specs for each item. That covers everything. All food, all drinks – everything. It even includes free samples that sales reps leave in for you to 'try out'. Again, your staff will believe they are doing you a favour because it's '100% profit' but your business should be a meticulously designed machine with everything placed and priced and positioned for a very specific reason. A few free high energy drinks by the next wannabe Red Bull or a box of cheap chocolate bars will upset this balance to a large extent.

Buying rules, training and very specific merchandising tactics (including photographs of the perfect set up) all need to be developed. Again this will take a little time at the beginning but it will also save you a lot of time, money and high blood pressure tablets in the future.

Johnny true story

There are three stories that I have to repeat ad nauseum.
I used to feel that I should be changing them on a regular
basis or that I was cheating readers or audience members
by telling these stories more than once. But I soon realised
that the reason why they're so important to me is that they were the big
epiphanies in my learning curve in terms of understanding how to run these
businesses. Each of the three stories individually represents more learning of
basic business sense than I got out of four full years studying business at
university.

Story one is the man in the brown suit (still the most important of all – see
page 27), story two was the grasping of responsibility story, and story three
(this one) is my 'systems' epiphany.

This story, like all great stories has a beginning, a middle, and an end. This
isn't because I paid particularly great attention at school in my English class (I
didn't) but because it took three main events to thoroughly drum the
information into my arrogant, thick, 'I know better' little brain.

Act I

Back in the sandwich bars days we had one great initial site. It made £45k of
net profit per year. With this in mind my business partner and I decided to
open a second site. We reasoned that if we made £45k in the first site, we
could do the same in a second site. We strutted around like a couple of junior
Richard Bransons and paid for a piece of research to be done in a little
satellite town outside Belfast where our existing shop was. This little town
had, what seemed to us, a similar socio-economic profile to the area around
our first site.

The research came back with a lot of fancy graphs and a lovely power point
presentation in a slick office with good coffee and great buns. It all looked
good. It would appear that our hunch was correct and it was potentially a
great location.

Armed with our fancy report, our cheap suits and slightly too shiny shoes, we
started looking for sites. I sat down one evening with the spreadsheet and

started to plan world domination through the medium of sandwich bars. I worked out my opening plan schedule and with each site providing £45k of income it certainly did look like 'this time next year . . . we'll be millionaires' or at some stage soon anyway.

We found a great site and put together our shiny new second shop. For a year we both ran around like mad men working very hard to run our two shops rather than just the one. Our egos grew at quite a rate but when we sat down with our accountants at the end of the year we had a bit of a shock. The new site hadn't been quite the instant success that we'd hoped for and had only made £15k in its first full year of trading. Also because we had taken our eye off the ball with the existing site we saw a profit fall. The £45k from the previous year turned into £30k. So the only benefit had been to our egos. We had worked twice as hard, increased our liabilities and yet were only making the same amount of money as we always had been. We were, to use another tired (but valid) industry cliché, 'busy fools'.

For the next site we knuckled down and started developing strong systems to ensure that the shops ran smoothly whether we were there or not.

Act II

After we sold off all our sandwich bars and stood penniless on the streets, we were at something of a loose end. A chance meeting with the friend of a friend produced an opportunity in the form of a recently closed fish and chip shop that had been granted a short lease to open again by the local council before they redeveloped the land. The appealing thing about the deal was that we didn't have to put up any money up front and could pay off the secondhand equipment over the term of the lease.

We opened the shop and split the work between us. My business partner would work the days and I would work the nights. It was hard and difficult work but I used it as a test bed for some of the ideas that had been occurring to me as I started to really grasp how business worked in the real world. During the day I would work 'on' the business and then, to pay the bills, would slog away at night serving food to the drinkers on their way home.

I developed systems to control theft and we religously produced weekly profit and loss accounts. If we felt there were any problems with our profitability we would even drop down to daily stock take and profit and loss reports to accurately work out exactly where the problem was. We created some strange marketing ideas and tested them along with playing with the menu to see how upmarket we could take it. Everything ran smoothly and by the end of the lease I felt it was time to delve a little deeper into testing these ideas and particularly the ideas of an American management thinker called Michael Gerber. Gerber had written a book called The 'E-myth' which was about the fundamental lack of understanding that most entrepreneurs operate within when they set up their business. He was a fan of creating a 'franchise model' of your business from day one.

We decided to apply this idea to a brand new fish and chip shop which we opened close by the old one. It was, as much as anything else, nothing more than a test bed for these ideas. The basic premise was that we were to produce a fish and chip shop with exceptional food and yet we would never work a single day in it ourselves. If we ended up being called in by the manager for a single shift, the experiment would be deemed a failure. The goal was ultimately to create a business that, to slightly paraphrase Michael Gerber's thinking, could be sold to a plumber who had no experience of the trade and could simply operate the system again without having to physically work within the business.

What that meant was an enormous amount of work before we ever opened the doors to serve a single portion of chips. We spent days perfecting the food but then the same amount of time creating the systems that meant it would be easily replicable on a consistent basis – and obviously without the need for expensive chefs. Everything from front door to back door was incorporated within a system and obviously from the very first week we had a rigorous weekly profit and loss system in place.

When we finally opened the doors the business was an instant success. During the first year we experimented (to great success) with our marketing systems and eventually about two years later we decided to move on. The business, as described elsewhere, was a huge success and we received numerous awards and press recognition for the quality of our food. But most important to us was the concept that our experiment had actually worked. We never worked a shift ourselves in those two years and ultimately actually did sell the business to a plumber. He kept the business for four years and it operated profitably throughout that time without him working a single shift himself. Occasionally he would go down to peel a few potatoes for them but never once did he get behind the counter.

Act III

The final act of this little play occurred a few years later. I was a director and shareholder in a multi-site large retail business with two very busy coffee shops. Initially most of my work had been towards the development of the first coffee shop. When we took it over it was operating in complete chaos and although the food was good it required a lot of work to make it consistently better. It took a while, and some considerable time, with a few key members of staff, but gradually it became a truly exceptional business. The systems and people development processes that we had put in place really paid off, and gradually I moved on towards the management and development of other aspects of the business.

But what had happened was that actually I had moved into classic working 'in' the business and the only reason I could leave the coffee shop to run so effectively was that it had been so effectively systemised by working 'on' it. I sat down with my day planner and calculated that I spent about three hours a week actively managing the coffee shop. It was the most profitable part of the enterprise and yet it took the least amount of time. The other parts of the business had become much harder to manage from a systems perspective because of differing opinions about how they should be operated.

From my own perspective it was all wrong. The lessons learnt in the previous two 'Acts' had been applied, but I was still working 'in' and 'doing a job' rather than creating a business that could work without me. The interesting thing for me though, was that the coffee shop had become what I now term a 'Three-hour business'. It was capable of running highly effectively and with almost no problems, on less than three hours input a week. That should be the ultimate goal for this type of business.

WHY YOUR BUSINESS NEEDS SYSTEMS

Those three Acts help to illustrate the somewhat painful process that you generally need to go through to accept that a business needs systems. Already I can hear people thinking 'well, that's not what I want, I don't want to spend three hours a week on my business. I don't want to spend all day on my boat, I'm doing this because I want to really be involved. I'm doing this because I have the first part of the formula – the passion – in abundance'.

The two are NOT mutually exclusive though. The key point is that it needs to be a choice. We're not saying that you need to remove yourself from the business as soon as possible, but we are saying that you must reach a stage where your involvement within the business is purely part of a lifestyle choice.

If you truly love working the coffee machine then it's absolutely fine to spend the majority of your day there in front of it in the same way that a fine chef who also owns the restaurant may want to spend much of his time creating and cooking in the kitchen. The key point is though that the business must be able to survive without you. If you break a leg it should be able to carry on quite happily and with the same level of profit.

Very often we meet clients who are trapped within their businesses and want out. They are looking for help with the sale and hope that we can come along and wave a magic wand to get them a huge price for it. The problem is that often these folk are the very people around whom the business totally revolves. They're the kind of people who hold all the information in their head and have their name above the door. For a purchaser that is incredibly unappealing. If the owner leaves there is little or nothing left of the business to carry forward. But as a purchaser if you can find a business that is profitable, strongly systemised and the owner has just returned from a three week safari in Africa, you have struck gold because the chances are that it can easily continue to generate these profits regardless of the ownership. It's exactly the same as the plumber buying the fish and chip shop.

So not only do you need strong systems to help you run and manage a great business, but you also need great systems to help you sell it.

SO WHAT EXACTLY NEEDS TO BE SYSTEMISED?

Well, the harsh reality of this is that it isn't quite as simple as wrapping a system around everything and then just sitting back and expecting it all to run smoothly. Within the coffee business you will find that your customers react very badly to a fast food mentality of 'would you like fries with that?', or by being herded like sheep from one section to another.

You need to find the balance between creating great systems to help manage the day-to-day functions of the business and also, through great training (and great initial recruitment), ensuring that your staff have the ability to think outside these systems when necessary, as well as allow their personality to shine through. This is not a particularly easy balance to strike.

The sorts of things that absolutely must be covered by a system are items such as:

- toilet cleaning rotas
- coffee machine cleaning
- opening routines
- closing routines
- rotas
- staffing systems (appraisals, disciplinary, grievance procedures etc.)
- food production
- food rotation
- cash procedures.

In an ideal world what you want to be doing is creating a 'brand manual' and an 'operations manual' before you actually open.

7 Money

Money is a quite remarkably complex part of the equation – not because so many people don't understand simple economics, but because so many people have a quite remarkably mixed up relationship with money. Countless years of indoctrination by poorly paid teachers, parents who lived through the war or didn't earn enough, and various social and political conditioning, very often leaves us thinking that money is, at heart, an evil thing that must be avoided if we don't want to burn in the pits of hell.

Sadly for you unless you can create a healthy relationship with money, you will end up burning in the pits of entrepreneurial hell – the bankruptcy court and that, trust us, is a very bad thing.

Café Culture

Great business fallacies number one – The international bureau of money distribution
This wonderful global organisation exists to redistribute the money and resources in the world in a 'fair manner'. It is a wonderful invention. The people that run it spend all day observing all the good and the bad people out there. They pay particular attention to all those folk running small businesses who 'work very hard'. After they have worked hard for a long time and done a 'really good job', they reward them with cold hard cash. They also observe all the lazy people who don't produce a great product but rely on good locations, slick marketing and fancy sales techniques to sell their products. They make certain that those people are punished and have their bottoms soundly thrashed.

The good people never get their bottoms thrashed – they will ultimately be rewarded with a nice comfy chair, lots of cash and a villa in Spain.

There's only one problem with this wonderful organisation – it doesn't exist. The only place it exists is in the imaginations of the millions of small business owners out there (and indeed hard working employees) who genuinely are doing a 'good job' but aren't currently being rewarded for it.

Sadly money (and indeed life) doesn't work that way and it never will – it isn't fair. The houses of good people burn down as often as the houses of bad people. Charity workers get run over by buses as often as rapists and murders. Neither the fire nor the bus driver makes a judgement on who to burn or run over.

Money makes no judgement either. If such an organisation did exist we would never have poverty and there would be no shortage of any essential items. All the houses and hotel buildings in places like Dubai and Las Vegas would have been instantly transferred to people who would never keep building houses and hotels in places like Las Vegas but would have instantly transferred all the cranes and builders to New Orleans after Hurricane Katrina.

If money was distributed fairly and for real value, people would never spend money on nonsense like Feng Shui, reality TV or gossip magazines that focus on the latest movements of footballers' wives.

Money moves to the celebrity and not necessarily to the most talented.

Additionally many of these small business owners have a concept of finite money. They have this fear and embarrassment that if they take a pound from a customer that this is one less pound they will have to spend on other essential goods. They get wrapped up in 'not wanting to rip the customer off' whilst sobbing gently at the end of each month as they realise, once again, that they really aren't making enough to pay the rent, let alone get a decent holiday.

People buy for all sorts of reasons and it is fundamentally NOT your business to judge them or worry about 'ripping them off' with an expensive cup of coffee of piece of cake. We all have different criteria for buying things, much of which is all wrapped up in all sorts of odd and deep social conditioning. If this wasn't the case then there would be no need for any premium brands at all. We'd all be driving around in Hyundais and nobody would be buying Mercedes, BMWs or even Fords. We'd all shop for all our food at the cheapest discount stores and nobody would contemplate eating or drinking products like champagne, foie gras or caviar.

Regardless of the economic situation, people spend money on what they regard as important and not what is necessarily right or even fair. The classic example of this is to drive through the absolutely worst neighbourhood near you and observe how many satellite TV aerials are stuck onto the walls outside. Peer through a few windows and observe just how big the TV is that is being watched inside. These items aren't cheap but they are what matters to the people who buy them. Their criteria are possibly different to yours or mine, but regardless of how little money they have they're still prioritising and making damn sure they have enough money to pay the satellite subscription every month.

The small business owner needs to stop relying on the IBMD and fight hard for some of the money that is out there. There will always be people who crave a good cup of coffee and it is your job to make really sure that they know about you and that you shout loudly and proudly about your brilliant product. Your lazy competitor up the street may have the better site and an inferior product but unless you do everything in your power to keep your business in the mind of the customer then he will get their ten or twenty pounds per week and not you. And unless you charge properly for what you sell you'll soon end up with no business at all.

SO HOW DOES THE WHOLE MONEY AND FINANCIAL THING WORK OUT?

Well, hopefully now that we've convinced you that it's actually okay to make a profit and perhaps, through our little visit to the bankruptcy court and the 'Man in the Brown suit' story, persuaded you just how easy it is to lose money and how deeply unpleasant it can be, we'd like to go through the basics again.

Our mantra in the first book was 'it's all about the money' and that's because so few owners (regardless of any odd personal relationships with money) actually struggle to make any. To a large extent this is due to ignorance. It's back to the whole heart surgeon analogy again, i.e. the heart surgeon only has to worry and focus his efforts on one little organ with four tubes coming out of it. The coffee shop owner has to juggle a huge variety of tasks, and the one that they tend to find most difficult to work with is the financial side. The whys and the wherefores of this are irrelevant – it just is. And if you find yourself in the group of potential owners (or existing owners) who struggle to fully grasp how it all adds up, we would really beseech you to pay attention to this part of the book, and to watch the accompanying video closely so that it's drilled into your brain.

Over the years (regardless of our own stupidity and naiveté) we have encountered the following expressions from clients, which they use to try and dismiss our pleas to focus on the numbers and understand their profit and loss sheet:

'Don't give me that percentage stuff – you always do that and I don't get it.'

'To be honest I tend to keep clear of the finances, that's not really my bag.'

'I've never understood a profit and loss and I never will. As long as I have enough money to pay the bills I'm happy.'

'Where does the VAT bit go?'

'Is net profit the same as gross profit?'

'My wage bill is about 50%. My accountant said that was okay but it seems a bit high to me?'

'What is a breakeven?'

'I don't care about the money. I just want to enjoy what I'm doing and if it makes a profit that's okay, if not that's fine.'

'Explain to me the difference between net sales and net profit again?'

The list is far from exhaustive but it does clearly show just how much the average (and in certain cases quite successful) coffee shop owner simply wants to ignore the whole financial side of the business.

The basic rules are as follows. It's vital that you watch the financials video on www.freecoffeeboys.com to understand this more easily but here it is in a nutshell.

First – some assumptions

Let's assume you have to pay sales tax (VAT in the UK) of 15%.

Let's assume that you've had a relatively busy day and that you have £1,150 in the till at the end of the day.

Let's assume you are in a relatively normal site with rent that isn't too cheap or too expensive.

Let's assume you make most of, but not all, products on site.

Let's assume you manage to keep your wage bill relatively tight.

So how much profit will you make that day?

Sales (or gross sales)	£1,150
VAT (to be paid directly to the VAT man each quarter)	£150
Net sales (after VAT deductions)	£1,000
Cost of sales (the actual cost to you of the goods you're selling)	£300
Gross profit	£700
Wage cost	£300
Contribution to overhead	£400

Overheads

Rent	£100
Rates	£50
General running costs (light, heat, uniforms, repairs etc.)	£100
Net profit (before interest depreciation and tax)	**£150**

How much money is left?

So that's it. Out of that £1,150 you have made about £150. Except you haven't. In most cases you'll probably be paying about another £100 towards the cost of originally setting up the business (depreciation) and on interest to pay the bank off, i.e. there is about £50 left over at the end of the day.

For some of you who are totally new to the business that is a big shock. You will probably have reached this stage in the book and thought that perhaps if you had done everything we said that you'd have a big financial success in your hands. Well that is possible but here are the facts.

Our clients range from making no money to putting about 20% to the bottom line, i.e. £200 out of that £1,150 figure above. Certain clients in very odd situations (within large corporations where various costs are hidden) make more than this but that isn't relevant to you because that is highly unlikely to be your situation.

The people who make no money or lose money either go out of business or we all work very hard to change a few key things and get them back on track. Those that make 20% (or in one case a fraction more) only do so by running a tight ship and having very small rent bills. They've also been at it a long time and usually don't have much to pay in the way of depreciation or interest to the banks.

But don't let this get you down. A good site can turn over in excess of £500,000 per annum and in certain cases can hit the million pound mark. That's rare but it is possible with the right site and without going down the restaurant route and opening every night.

If you can put 20% to the bottom line of a £500,000 site you're doing well and could be making (in addition to any reasonable salary you may take out if you physically work there) somewhere in the region of £100,000 of profit every year. Stack a few sites together like that (obviously not as easy as it sounds) and you have a really serious business.

But that is the exception. You are more likely to make somewhere between 5% and 15% net profit and that's what you should be basing your initial projections on.

Not prepared to believe that?

Well we decided to drag a good client in to explain to you in his words what the most important part of the business is. This client currently has 12 sites and has been through pretty much all the pitfalls in the rest of the formula (as we all have) but has come out the far side with a great business.

Here are his thoughts on the money side of things:

Know your numbers

When it comes to the crunch, if you don't know the basic numbers and you just follow your heart or your ego over your head, you could very quickly come unstuck.

My golden rules

Rent. Sales must be 10% and must be achievable in a very short space of time. Starbucks have struggled in the UK because they are at 25% rent:sales. They have focused on ego and fancy high street retail pitches. The problem is they sell coffee not diamond rings.

Stick to a ceiling rental level and don't be tempted to squeeze above it. My ceiling is currently £50,000.

Then, as a broad rule of thumb, establish what your daily target is, in terms of cup sales and absolute sales, to make a living.

In this example, 686 cups of coffee per day and £1,374 will produce a solid return (assuming gross margin is circa 70% and wage:sales is contained under 28%). If you push your rental levels much higher than this and your core business is coffee, you will struggle to retain product quality. We try very hard to produce silky smooth texture across our drinks. This requires highly polished milk and passionate baristas. I don't feel this would be possible if you had to run much harder. And when you compromise on product quality the top line starts to disappear.

Fit out must not exceed the rent-free period. Always push for a three-month rent free period or you face a leaking tap from day 1.

Wage: Should not exceed 26% of sales. Manage this in a three-stage process – weekly, daily and hourly. Don't rest on your laurels of a weekly rota which is static. Remember two hours saved every day, for just three days a week is £2,000 a year – straight from your bottom line.

Gross margin: One percent change in gross profit is a 30% change in net profit. This statistic says it all.

The hardest concept to fully grasp is gross margin. But ignore it at your peril. Establish all the drivers behind gross margin: wastage, theft, delivery receiving procedures, stocktake discipline etc . . . All these factors need to be in check.

Communicate the numbers: The sooner you can pull individuals into the real game of business, the better. Establish the core drivers and communicate accordingly. Drip feed store level information relating to wage:sales and sales weekly. Drip feed gross margin monthly.

If you don't tell your people the numbers they will generally make them up. And you can guarantee their numbers will be much higher than yours.

Communicate the big numbers as soon as you have them to all your people. Empower people and reward people.

Plan the numbers: Always have a target for your business numbers, at a store and group level 12 months in advance. And monitor every month whether you are over or under performing against these.

James Shapland – Managing Director Coffee #1

We couldn't have put it any better ourselves.

To see a full working explanation of a profit and loss for a sample coffee shop make sure you check out the resources at www.coffeeboysguide.com

Part Four

Step-by-step Action Plan

A STEP-BY-STEP WALK THROUGH THE WEEKS AND MONTHS IN THE LEAD UP TO OPENING A COFFEE SHOP

So you've decided to get going. You've made the big decision and had the awkward chat with your husband/wife/boss/children – now exactly how are you going to string it all together?

The timeframe required to open a coffee shop can vary enormously between sites and the various models that you might be talking about. In the right situation, you could have something up and running in a matter of days or weeks but for other situations it could take years. There simply is no right or wrong time to spend on getting going, but the key thing is to keep going relentlessly. Once you've made the commitment you need to forge forward and blast through the obstacles.

STEP ONE – DECIDING ON THE MODEL

What exactly will you be doing? Will you be a Starbucks clone or a homely old-fashioned coffee house with an emphasis on food?

For the purposes of this example let's assume that we're dealing with a small coffee shop off the main high street in a reasonably sized town. At www.freecoffeeboys.com we have produced a project plan (using exactly the same system that we use for proper businesses) detailing the process for this fictional business.

So once you have settled on the model you then need to decide where you'll be based.

Hugo true story – The Communicator

I know, like everybody, that one of the biggest issues with all businesses and organisations is 'Communication'. It's probably the biggest issue in any kind of relationship. If the communication is good then the relationship is great but if the relationship is not good or is in difficulty, then you can assume that lack of communication is a major factor.

We all know this but rarely do much about it. In our business we service all our customers' coffee equipment and it is a significant logistical operation. There are four service engineers all with different strengths and specific areas of expertise and there are hundreds of customers with a large geographic spread. Naturally when a customer encounters a problem it is the only one that matters to them and they all expect us to drop everything immediately and tend to their specific problem as they can't sell coffee without their equipment working.

Years ago our business ran like everybody else's and we were as good and as bad as everybody else. One day my car broke down and I had several urgent appointments. I rang my dealer cover and was put through to Alison who owned the problem immediately. She understood the urgency, was able to talk about the electrics in my car with knowledge (and was careful to say that she needed the expert's opinion), took all the details quickly and said she would come back to me in no more than ten minutes. Seven minutes later she called to say that the RAC was on their way and as she realised it was urgent, she had arranged a loan car at the dealership nearby if I was able to return it.

Not everything was perfect about this solution, but it came close – so we used the best of this experience with Alison and created a Helpdesk with an Operational Manager whose main role was to communicate what was happening to our customer to our service and training departments and our sales people. This focus on the customer – simply by very accurately keeping them informed – transformed our business and we gained a fantastic reputation for service excellence, even though we were servicing the machines and calls in a very similar fashion. It was the good communication that created the perceived improvement.

STEP TWO – DECIDING WHERE YOU'LL BE BASED

This is clearly based on the model we've discussed in the location section. The key thing is to be realistic about what you can or cannot do in various sites. If you find a magnificent site which may appeal to a model that is slightly different to what your dream is, then you must make commercial decisions. Bring a wrong model to the wrong market and you have a disaster on your hands. So be flexible and prepare to tweak according to the site and model that you've chosen. For our fictional site we'll assume there is no tweaking though.

STEP THREE – DECIDING WHETHER TO RENT OR LEASE

There are pros and cons of each and one isn't necessarily faster or better than the other. Unless you have large amounts of capital you're likely to end up leasing. At this stage you'll need to be engaging with the first of the various advisors that you'll be coming in contact with.

You'll need to be dealing with estate agents and whilst it's a wonderful cliché to follow the herd and hate these people, that's a huge mistake. You should be regularly keeping in contact with them and making sure that they're on your side. Yes their job is to try to sell you the benefits of various sites but you also want them to contact YOU first when the best sites become available. They'll also need to potentially 'sell' you to the landlord so it's highly advisable that you don't treat them like something you stepped on.

If you have an existing site you will generate enormous brownie points with your local agents by some strategically delivered free coffee and buns on a Friday, i.e. there is a game to be played here – make sure you play it correctly.

At this stage too you need to start thinking about lawyers. Your best solution is always to go with personal recommendations if possible. And again be aware that your lawyer should be someone that you keep on your side – these guys are expensive and you need to get every ounce of value possible from them. But you also need to be aware that they are going to be very cautious. Most lawyers can manage to find half a dozen items in every lease that put the fear of god in them. If you're very cautious you'll never get your shop open so the time for pig-headed determination and a healthy dose of pragmatism has arrived, i.e. take all your lawyers advice, change what you can with the lease, and then take a commercial decision yourself whether to go ahead or not. In certain situations this may even involve going against the advice of your lawyer but that's okay as long as your eyes are wide open.

Sadly though you cannot adopt a 'Oh I'll never understand a legal document with all that fancy language' attitude. Yes it's your lawyer's job to go through it but you also need to go through the whole document too. You may well not fully grasp all the points but by re-reading sentences two or three times they become surprisingly easy to interpret.

Your final advisor at this stage should be your accountant. Again you really want to seek someone out who has experience of this type of business and is recommended personally. It sounds ludicrous but many accountants simply do not fully grasp the intricate details of a coffee shop accounts. They may not have ever worked with one before and this is a potential disaster for you.

STEP FOUR – PUTTING TOGETHER YOUR PROJECTED PROFIT AND LOSS

Once you have identified your site you need to sit down and start to work out the figures that relate to that unit. It depends a little on how you're going to fund the business but you need to put together a projected profit and loss and cashflow for the first year. If you require bank funding then this is the stage you need to make the visit. If you aren't familiar with producing these yourself then you'll need to sit down with your accountant and work them out.

We have a downloadable profit and loss projection available for you at the www.coffeeboysguide.com website. This allows you to slot in a variety of different turnover, rent, wage and cost of sales scenarios so that you can accurately have an idea of how much or how little you might make.

At this stage it's crucial to firmly remove the rose-tinted spectacles and really look at the worst-case scenarios. Limit yourself to a five-minute session with a cup of coffee and perhaps a bourbon biscuit as you dream about the best-case scenario. Over the years we have both been caught up in the 'look at that – we'll make millions out of this' scenario and we still see it almost every week in life for new clients. Please make sure you are as realistic as possible here.

A good way to play this 'game' properly is to create a totally realistic scenario (in your own mind) and then apply a few 'what ifs?' to it. Assume that your sales are 20% lower because any number of things might have gone wrong. Now assume that it takes you a good year to get on top of your wage costs and increase your wage percentages by that same percentage. Finally, assume that your food costs are a lot harder to control (or that there is a major increase in actual supply costs) and increase those figures by 3%. If you still have a business that works for you then you can feel a little comfortable with that. If not, then it's time for a very serious sit down and 'chat' with yourself.

Below we have an example of this. Please be aware that we are NOT accountants and that different banks or accountants will present this information in different ways. Please also be aware that these figures are not something that you should expect for your business. Each business is totally unique. Many of the same rules must apply but there will be subtle differences in every one, i.e. we do not want emails saying 'you told me that my rates should be about £9,000 in your book and that my electricity bill should be only six grand!'

Scenario 1

Scenario 1		
Sales (less VAT)	200,000	
Cost of sales	60,000	*30%*
Gross profit	140,000	
Wages (inc. partners and NIC)	60,000	*30%*
Contribution to overhead	80,000	
Overheads		
Rent	20,000	
Rates	9,000	
Marketing	6,000	
Gas, electricity	6,000	
Phone, stationery, postage	3,000	
Accountancy/bookeeping	2,000	
Insurance	2,000	
Bank charges	0	
Travel/motoring expenses	4,000	
Sundries	4,000	
Total overheads	56,000	
Depreciation	20,000	
Interest	5,000	
Net profit	19,000	

As you can see in scenario 1 there is a reasonable profit at the end of the year. The partners have been paid within the wage cost (and at this level of wages we would assume that they are working in a hands on way) and we have also assumed that the bank has allowed a year free of charges. We have also tentatively assumed a deprecation charge of £20,000 based on £100,000 over five years.

It all looks relatively okay. Our fictional partners can look at a turnover increase for year two and can start planning that holiday in the Maldives. They can also briefly fall into the trap of thinking 'imagine if we had ten of those!'

Scenario 2

Scenario 2

Sales (less VAT)	160,000	
Cost of sales	52,800	33%
Gross profit	107,200	
Wages (inc. partners and NIC)	52,800	33%
Contribution to overhead	54,400	
Overheads		
Rent	20,000	
Rates	9,000	
Marketing	6,000	
Gas, electricity	6,000	
Phone, stationery, postage	3,000	
Accountancy/bookkeeping	2,000	
Insurance	2,000	
Bank charges	0	
Travel/motoring expenses	4,000	
Sundries	4,000	
Total overheads	56,000	
Depreciation	20,000	
Interest	5,000	
Net Profit	−6,600	

Scenario two is a little different however and much, much more likely to actually be the case (based on our experience with many, many start-ups.) Here the turnover is 20% less than previously estimated and the wage and cost of sales figures are up 3% each.

Suddenly the profit looks more like a small but significant loss.

This is where you need to be totally realistic.

■ Exactly what would this mean to you?

■ How much spare cash would you have to plug such a hole?

■ What if it happened for a couple of years?

■ What would you do to ensure this didn't happen?

■ What brave decisions would you make if it did happen?

■ What spare cash would you have to put into marketing or perhaps a change of layout?

Again it's crucial to really imagine yourself in that situation. It's an extremely common occurrence and what most operators do is simply put the 'head down' so far that they become an ostrich in the sand and work more and more hours and become more and more disillusioned.

The key point here once again is realism – not realism in the sense that this WILL happen but a realistic view of what could happen and how you might deal with it. With that sense of realism intact you can then much more clearly move forward and not just jump in with a strong sense of 'Just get me out of this tedious job I'm in – I don't care how much money it makes me!'

STEP FIVE – WRITING A BUSINESS PLAN

You'll also need to put together a basic business plan at this stage too. Business plans are essential as a guide to get you going but you should be aware that they will almost immediately become worthless as the business takes a few changes of direction within the first few months. You can also completely forget the notion that a good plan with a fancy cover will help you with the bank.

A bank manager will only really be interested in three things:

■ How much money you need and where is it coming from.

■ What you are prepared to put up as collateral (i.e. if the business goes bust what personal assets can they grab).

■ What your cashflow looks like (they will look through this for any obvious flaws).

They will completely ignore any research you have done and any fancy charts or marketing plans. It's frustrating, but as long as you can bear this in mind you can then use it to your advantage – forewarned is forearmed so to speak.

Steps one to five will have taken a few months to sort so we can now assume that everything has gone well and you have a signed lease in your nervous little hand.

Johnny true story

When I first arrived in the world of entrepreneurial activity, I was fresh faced and clutching a business degree certificate under my arm. At university we had all learnt how to do business plans and therefore as we decided to expand our little sandwich business from one site to two, I confidently produced a business plan of immense beauty. We had spent (pointlessly in hindsight) a reasonable amount of money with a market research firm and had a quite staggering amount of facts and figures in this wonderful plan.

Ultimately we didn't really want very much money and with the success of the first site we were very confident that the bank would put up all the money for the new one. We made our appointment with the manager and dusted off the 'funeral and bank manager' suit and tie.

The day came and I confidently placed the plan down on his desk with a few spare copies available for others. It was then that I was introduced to a somewhat brutal reality. It was a harsh reality that I was to witness many times with many different ventures over the years. The reality was:

He turned to the back page . . .

That's what 'they' do. All they're interested in is three things:

1. How much do you want?
2. What have you got to put up against it?
3. How easily can you pay it back?

And those three things will be covered at the end of your plan. This doesn't mean you should ignore the plan but be very aware of what it is for. Ultimately it really is for you. It's for you to crystallise the concept in your mind and make sure you know exactly what the various scenarios are likely to be. It's to force you to come up with a decent marketing plan and calendar for the year. It's to force you to really think about this business and exactly how you're going to run it.

Needless to say we didn't get the money and had to scrabble it together from a variety of other sources including the oft-used 'car loan'.

So what should be in a plan? Most UK banks have lots of advice in this area and it's often worthwhile to find the relevant information that your bank has before approaching them for help. This way your plan can be created from their model and they're less likely to be confused when you present something to them in a different format. We also have a draft plan available at the website but in essence you need to focus on the following.

An executive summary

This will contain the basic outline of what it is that you're proposing. This is a crucial part of the plan because it's the only part that has a small chance of being read by the banks or investors other than the financials. So do this after you have completed everything else and make really sure that it is crystal clear and not full of woolly guff that they won't be interested in. This should not be any more than a page.

Business structure

Here is where you go into the details of who you are and exactly what you and your partners have that makes you qualified to be opening a business like this. Here you need to go into the details of partnerships and shareholdings. You also need to formulate in crystal clear terms exactly what the key people will be doing. Again you should be aware that this is more for you than for the bank but it is an incredibly important exercise to help you out in the future. We see a tremendous amount of businesses experience difficulties because of a lack of clarity between partners in the initial stages. It can stifle growth and be tremendously damaging to the business even before it has had a chance to get going.

Business overview

Exactly what it is that you will be doing? Full details of all products and where the business will be located. The opening hours, the competition, the revenue sources and an in depth analysis and understanding of how it all works and will come together needs to be clearly articulated here.

Once more this exercise is for you as much as for the bank. It forces you to be incredibly realistic about the business and how it will work. But again you must be totally realistic. If at this stage of the plan you find little chinks in the armour of your 'wonderful idea', you need to delve very deep into those 'chinks' and find out if they are a real problem or something that can be tweaked and adjusted into a more commercial model.

You should also use evidence based on your research here but not the full research itself. Any research should be kept in an appendix at the back. What we're after here are cold hard facts – not lovely graphs and statistics.

Marketing

How are you going to persuade the public that what you do is great? Are you going to sit back and do a Field of Dreams – 'if you build it they will come?' – because anyone who has watched Wayne's World II knows that this may not actually be the case.

Once more our slightly tedious friend 'Mr Realism' needs to make an appearance. The marketing of your business is an absolutely crucial part of the potential success or failure and you must make sure that you have it properly planned out AND costed.

Operations

How are you going to manage it? Who will do what? What equipment will be used? How will it all come together? What will happen on a day-to-day basis?

You also need to include full details of how you will recruit, train and retain your new employees. A people plan that includes you, your Aunt Sadie and your mother-in-law will cause any potential investors or bankers to have a kitten.

You should also list all your major suppliers and key relationships at this stage.

Financials

This is the really important bit. You need three main elements here:

1. How much it will cost to put it together (and how this will be funded).

2. A cashflow for the first year.

3. Your projected profit and loss for the first year.

A useful and incredibly important rule of thumb is to add 30% onto the actual cost of opening your shop as the extra amount you will need to get you through the first year. Most new starts come up with a figure to open their store and it covers everything to get the doors open and very little else. Usually this figure is the total amount they have available and they then expect to be 'raking it in' during the first few weeks. Needless to say this rarely happens.

The 30% covers you for a little overspend and all the inevitable things that you've forgotten about or have to change in the first few weeks. It also provides you with a small cushion should things not be quite as busy as you had first expected.

Ninety per cent of you will ignore that piece of advice (we did ourselves to begin with) but it will make your life vastly easier if you can pull together that extra bit of money (or at least have access to it) and can, in certain situations, be the difference between success and failure.

STEP SIX – PULLING TOGETHER ALL YOUR SUPPLIERS

You need about three months at this stage (again this can vary enormously). Now you want to be pulling together the following groups of people:

- coffee suppliers
- crockery suppliers
- disposable suppliers
- savoury product suppliers
- bun offer suppliers
- chefs/cooks if you intend to produce your offer in house
- builders/shop fitters
- catering equipment suppliers (must be able to work closely with the above)
- soft drink suppliers
- local newspaper journalists

- baristas

- general counter staff

- managers

- shift supervisors

- till suppliers

- signage manufacturers.

The key factors (as you will see on the project plan) are shop fitting times and staffing. It will generally take the full three months to recruit a decent team around you and allow them enough time to work out notice or holidays.

During this stage you need your very best pig-headed determination face on. Almost without exception you will be bombarded daily by concept diluters and suppliers who promise the earth but let you down. It's your job to keep strong and not compromise unless you really have to. It's incredibly tiring but also absolutely crucial to the success of your business.

STEP SEVEN – OPEN THE DOORS!

Launches are to be avoided at all costs. When you open you don't want to be putting too much pressure on your shiny new business. Get a few days under your belt in a relatively quiet fashion and then start to crank up your marketing. Often the most effective way to drive a lot of traffic in is to give away a lot of food but be very, very careful about this if your team is inexperienced and likely to collapse under pressure.

Once open your job in the first few weeks is to systemise everything. Every problem should be listed down and a system created to cover it as soon as possible. Once you have some sense of control you then need to crank up the marketing. So your emphasis must shift as soon as possible from working *in* to working *on*.

So that's it – your business is open and hopefully you've followed the formula and will soon be reaping the rewards.

Make sure you check out www.coffeeboysguide.com for further information.

Coffeeboys useful contacts

You may have heard of our five 20s concept in the business of coffee. It came about during a long discussion over several days on a coffee roasters tour of the West Coast of America from Seattle down though Olympia, Portland, Grant's Pass (notably the town with the most drive thru's in the US), Santa Rosa to San Francisco with the infamous Coffeehunter Stephen Hurst.

We agreed essentially that the coffee business was made up of five main sectors: **Farmers** and everything to do with growing, harvesting, processing and production; **Green**, which is basically the selection, buying, shipping and selling of fine coffee from origin; **Roasting**, which obviously includes every combination and option; **Distribution and Equipment**, which includes the significant business of selling, training, marketing, branding and the enormous area of equipment; and the **Barista**, which is basically delivery of the end product and retailing.

What we found particularly interesting about these five sectors was that each one believes that theirs is the most important. But the real truth is that actually – for a great coffee offer you have to get each one right and they are interdependent. We can see where many companies have attempted to vertically integrate this process in order to squeeze extra margin, and while that is indeed an ideal to work towards, in practice, because there is so much to each of these sectors, it is almost impossible to do more than two well.

With that in mind we have put together a list of companies and contacts that we believe are the best in the world in each broad sector. Clearly this list is not exhaustive and there are many great companies out there that we have not yet come across. Your job is to find the right partners for your business. It is also the case that this list is undoubtedly UK and US biased as this is where we have spent most of our time.

ORIGIN/FARMERS

Mountain Top, New South Wales, Australia

www.mountaintopcoffee.com/au

Andrew Gold is a breath of fresh air and delivers his message with typical gusto. Has great coffee, a great story and great passion. Always worth a look.

Fazenda Fortaleza, San Sebastiao do Paraiso, Brazil

www.bsca.com.br/intertech_br.html

Alex Nogueira Frossard is the poster boy of the BSCA! An ex President of the organisation and a fantastic ambassador for Brazilian speciality coffee. Now roasting his own coffee as well we hear.

Bourbon Specialty Coffees, Pocos de Caldas, Brazil

www.bourboncoffees.com.br

Gabriel de Carvalho Dias and his cousin Cristiano Ottoni have established one of the finest quality exporting operations from Brazil. Gabriel was one of the founders of BSCA and frequent winner of the Brazil Cup of Excellence. His fabulous attention to detail is the hallmark of his great coffee and has been at the forefront in raising standards and quality of fine Brazils.

Cambraia Cafes, Fazenda Samambia, San Antonio do Amparo, Brazil

www.cambraiacafes.com.br

Henrique Dias Cambria owns Samambia and manages a co-operative in San Antonio where he produces consistently great coffee every year. He is one of the nicest guys in the business and one to trust.

Daterra Coffee, Campinas, São Paulo, Brazil

www.daterracoffee.com.br

Technology, research and attention to the environment during coffee production has led Daterra to become known as one of the best coffee producers in the world and the choice of many barista champions.

Finca La Perla, Guatemala

www.fincalaperla.com

Multiple award winner at Cup of Excellence. Owned by the Arenas family and managed by Christian Schaps. A classic estate from the Quiche region of Guatemala.

GREEN

Mercanta The Coffee Hunters

www.coffeehunter.com

Stephen Hurst along with his business partner Flori Martin and their dedicated team are, in our opinion, the global leaders in unique and individual speciality coffee lots. They strive to deliver on their robust principles and always do what they say. These are the guys for something special.

Vinco Sandali, Trieste, Italy

Sandali Trading Company is based in Trieste, where it brings together a long family tradition in commerce. They are importers and blenders of fine coffees for the original Italian espresso blend.

Schluter SA, Nyon Switzerland

Supplies Africa's best coffees from all across the continent! Trading office based just outside Geneva in Switzerland, Schluter SA have been present in Africa since the early days of commercial coffee production.

ROASTERS

Stumptown Coffee, Portland

www.stumptowncoffee.com

Run by the unique Dwain Sorenson and a really fantastic business to visit. Several sites in Portland and a strong wholesale divison. Passionate about great coffee and with a great spirit.

Intelligentsia Coffee, Chicago, US

www.intelligentsiacoffee.com

This business is a great example of how to create a culture and build a great team. Led and inspired by Doug Zell, it is based in Chicago with another roasting works in LA. Stores are in Chicago, LA, Venice, and a Lab in New York. Strong wholesale business and real innovators. Ireland's 2008 World Barista Champion, Stephen Morrissey is their Head of Training.

Counter Culture, Durham, NC

www.counterculturecoffee.com

Another of the cutting-edge roasters from the US. We love its strap line 'We are not trying to change the world, just the way it thinks about coffee'.

Terrior Coffee Company, Acton, MA

www.terroircoffee.com

George Howell is one of the coffee world's most knowledgeable and passionate spokesmen. He has long list of achievements including co-founding The Cup of Excellence. His latest company, Terrior, produces coffee that is as good as you can get.

Monmouth Coffee Company, London

www.monmouthcoffee.com

Operating since the 70s, this is an extraordinary coffee company with a couple of fabulous stores in London's Covent Garden and Borough Market (our favourite). The first we know to pioneer single serve origin coffees. They supply many of London's best coffee bars. On top of all that, we love Angela Holder.

Square Mile Coffee Roasters, London

www.squaremilecoffeeroasters.com

Run by World Champions James Hoffman and Annette Moldvaer, this company is at the cutting edge of UK coffee roasting. It continually raises the bar in the coffee it sources, the quality its staff deliver through a clever selective sell approach, and the challenges it provides for the bigger boys who have been in their comfort zone for years.

Hasbean, Brighton

www.hasbean.com

Steve Leighton is charismatic and great fun. He also works so hard at every detail of his coffee business demonstrated by his website, blog and twitters. This website is ideal for experimenting with great coffees at home. Reliable delivery – including Sunderland!

Peter James Gourmet Coffee

www.jamesgourmetcoffee.com

Peter is one of the best roasters in the UK coffee world. Massive experience and knowledge and truly remarkable coffee.

Coffee Compass

www.coffeecompass.co.uk

Richard Janz is a great roaster who delivers fantastic coffee with great service. Based in the West Country, he has been around a long time and is one of life's good guys. We have had many laughs and good times with Richard.

Union Coffee Roasters, London

www.unionroasted.com

Owned and run by Jeremy Torz and Steven Maccatonia, these two are legendary in the coffee world having sold their original business to Starbucks and then set up Union – coffee with a conscience. Always worth keeping an eye on.

Matthew Algie, Glasgow

www.matthewalgie.com

Built into an innovative coffee business by the late David Williamson who will be badly missed. Supply chain includes large hotel groups, Marks & Spencer, and Pret.

Bewleys Coffee, Dublin

www.bewleys.com

Ireland's point of reference and market leader. Almost anybody who is anybody in the Irish coffee scene has been through Bewleys, and it deserves great credit for its stickability. Paul O'Toole is one of the most experienced coffee (and tea) men in the world and a brilliant 1-to-1 teacher. Don't miss any opportunity you may get with him.

Contra Coffee, Copenhagen

www.contracoffee.com

Set up by a trio of World Barista Champions, Contra has innovated and led the Scandanavian coffee scene with some fine coffees and superb blends. We also rate Troels Poulson at the top end of world coffee expert communicators.

Robert Thoresen, Mocca Kaffebar & Brenneri, Norway

Robert Thoresen, 2002 World Champion, runs his dynamic roasting business in Norway and excudes enormous passion and care for what he does. A very special treat to visit his stores in Oslo . . . a treat if you are ever there.

DISTRIBUTORS/TRAINERS/EQUIPMENT

Distributors

Darlingtons, London

www.darlingtonscoffee.com

Successful and niche coffee distribution company in London with many first rate and prestigious customers.

Peros, High Wycombe, Bucks

www.peros.co.uk

The kings of the Midlands. Innovative, experienced with a comprehensive service.

Clifton Coffee, Bristol

Highly regarded Bristol-based coffee distributors.

Specialist Beverages, Northern Ireland

www.specialistbeverages.com

Set up and owned by our very own Hugo and brother James. Brilliant – need we say more!

Training and consultancy

London School of Coffee

www.londonschoolofcoffee.com

This is an outstanding coffee training business with superb facilities in Kingston upon Thames, UK.

Espresso Logic, Belfast

Hugo's coffee consultancy and training business. Brilliant again . . . particularly Sharon Magowan!

Insturator, Australia

www.espressoquest.com

There is only one Insturator that's for sure. Inspiring and unique in every way. Their book is fantastic.

Jon Willasen, Barcelona, Spain

Jon is probably the best cupping trainer we have ever come across. Currently based in Spain, he can be found at the big annual events (SCAE and SCAA) teaching and lecturing and is unmissable.

Bellisimo, USA

www.espresso101.com

A great site with loads of experience and some great products and advice.

Equipment

La Cimbali, Milan, Italy

www.cimbali.com

Highly respected brand and light years ahead of the pack with fully automatics.

La Marzocco, Florence, Italy

www.lamarzocco.com

Legendary traditional kit with a long world barista championship (WBC) pedigree and following around the world.

La Spaziale, Bologna, Italy

www.laspaziale.com

Fantastically reliable and credible company with a real heritage and depth of experience.

Dalla Corte, Milan, Italy

www.dallacorte.com

One of the new and innovative manufacturers making a name for itself at the top end.

Bunnomatic, US, Europe, and the world

www.bunn.com

As far as filter coffee brewing goes, these guys set the benchmark. Wide range, serious resource and world players.

Marco, Dublin

www.marco.ie

Led by the inspirational Paul Stack, continually innovating and driving market changing concepts. One to watch.

BARISTAS/RETAILERS

There are so many great retailers and baristas, that it would be unfair to try and produce a comprehensive list. We argued (or perhaps more accurately bickered) over this list at great length and then had moments of panic when we realised just how many people we might miss out.

The other problem is that this is easily the most fluid part of the business. Great coffee shops and baristas come and go. Therefore it's the part of this list that most obviously lends itself to a web presence. So at the www.coffeeboysguide.com site, please make sure you read our most up to date list but also put up your own recommendations and that way we can keep the list current.

Associations and others

Speciality Coffee Association of Europe

www.scae.com

Speciality Coffee Association of Brazil

www.bsca.com.br

Speciality Coffee Association of Japan

www.scaj.com

Cup of Excellence

www.cupofexcellence.com

Speciality Coffee Association of America

www.scaa.org

Caffe Culture, UK

www.cafeculture.com

And don't forget to go to www.coffeeboysguide.com and to check out the videos that accompany this book.

Index

Wake up
and smell the
52 profit

GUARANTEED
WAYS...

...TO MAKE

MORE MONEY

IN YOUR

COFFEE

BUSINESS

*'A quite brilliant
new book on
cafe operation.'*
COFFEE HOUSE MAGAZINE

John Richardson & Hugh Gilmartin

Also by John Richardson and Hugh Gilmartin

WAKE UP AND SMELL THE PROFIT

52 guaranteed ways to make more money in your coffee business

Witty, authoritative, comprehensive and fun, *Wake Up and Smell the Profit* is the ultimate guide to making more money in your coffee business.

With 52 motivating tips and suggestions (plus an extra bonus idea for good measure), all you need to do is apply one initiative a week for a year and you could have a much more profitable and easier to manage business within twelve months.

With this book you'll be able to:

■ Make more money and work less

■ Have happier customers who spend more money

■ Win more customers without spending a fortune

■ Enjoy running your business more

■ Create customers who rave about your business and consequently generate more customers through word of mouth

ISBN 978-1-84528-334-6   £9.99

START AND RUN A DELICATESSEN

DEBORAH PENRITH

This book will tell you all you need to know to start and run your own delicatessen shop, including choosing the right location; researching your market; writing a business plan and raising finance; how to market your business and attract customers; managing food hygiene and health and safety; how to employ and manage your staff; how to advertise cost effectively; keeping the accounts and handling VAT; and sourcing organic food direct from the farmer, or at markets or trade shows. And once you're up and running it will tell you how to expand your business into other areas such as catering to businesses and private functions and assembling and delivering gift hampers.

ISBN 978-1-84528-314-8

WORK FROM HOME

How to make money working at home – and get the most out of life

JUDY HEMINSLEY

Whether you are planning to run your own business or work from home as an employee for a large company, you will share experiences and be looking for solutions to similar challenges. This is a down-to-earth, practical and friendly guide, designed to help you get the best out of working from home. It includes lots of options to help you choose and develop the arrangements that best suit you and your family. In it you'll discover: whether you and your work are suited to working from home; how to negotiate homeworking with your employer; how to maintain a professional image; how to separate work from home; and much more.

ISBN 978-1-84528-335-3

START AND RUN AN INTERNET BUSINESS

CAROL ANN STRANGE

'An excellent definitive guide.' *Jobs & Careers*

This book will guide you through the process of establishing a profitable online venture and steer you towards success. You'll learn how to generate inline income; create a reliable and appealing virtual shop window; optimise your web venture for growth; generate more profit from affiliate schemes and other prospects and become a successful internet entrepreneur.

ISBN 978-1-84528-356-8

MASTERING BOOK-KEEPING

DR PETER MARSHALL

An accredited textbook of The Institute of Chartered Bookkeepers.

This updated 8th edition contains extracts from ICB, AAT, OCR and AQA sample examination papers.

'This book has been planned to cover the requirements of all the major examining boards' syllabuses and achieves all it sets out to do.' *Focus on Business Education*

'Presented in a clear and logical manner – written in plain English.' *Learning Resources News*

'This book has great potential value.' *Educational Equipment Magazine*

ISBN 978-1-84528-324-7

WRITING A WINNING BUSINESS PLAN

MATTHEW RECORD

'This book will not only help you prepare a business plan but will also provide a basic understanding of how to start up a business.' – *Working from Home*

'An excellent reference for even the most inexperienced business person looking to march into the business world ably armed with a professional plan.' – *Home Business Alliance*

ISBN 978-1-84528-302-5

THE SMALL BUSINESS START-UP WORKBOOK

CHERYL D. RICKMAN

'I would urge every business adviser in the land to read this book' – Sylvia Tidy-Harris, Managing Director of **www.womenspeakers. co.uk**

'Inspirational and practical workbook that takes you from having a business idea to actually having a business. By the time you have worked through the exercises and checklists you will be focussed, confident and raring to go.' – **www.allthatwomenwant.co.uk**

'A real 'must have' for anyone thinking of setting up their own venture.' – *Thames Valley News*

'. . . a very comprehensive book, a very readable book.' – *Sister Business E-Zine*

ISBN 978-1-84528-038-3

SETTING UP & RUNNING A LIMITED COMPANY

ROBERT BROWNING

'Many businesses are run though companies but there are legal implications, and careful consideration required before forming a limited company. This guide sets out the pros and cons, and how to proceed.' – *Landlordzone.co.uk*

ISBN 978-1-85703-866-8

HOW TO GET FREE PUBLICITY

PAM AND BOB AUSTIN

This step-by-step manual is ideal for for small businesses, clubs, schools or charities. In it you'll discover how to present stories that will get accepted by editors and how to write effective press releases and articles and deal with media interviews.

ISBN 978-1-84528-180-9

85 INSPIRING WAYS TO MARKET YOUR SMALL BUSINESS

JACKIE JARVIS

This book sets out some great ideas and explains how each idea will benefit your business, what you need to do to make it work, and how you can apply it to your own business *immediately*.

ISBN 978-1-84528-396-4

PREPARE TO SELL YOUR COMPANY

L B Buckingham

Selling your company is a trying time, similar to selling your house. For those unfamiliar with this process, the challenging thoughts will be: 'How do I start?'; 'Who can help me?'; 'How much can I get for the business?'; 'Who is most likely to buy it, and where do I find them?'; 'When should I do it?' This book will answer all your questions. Easy to read, it covers all the practical aspects of preparing your business for sale. It will show you just how a potential acquirer will view a company that is up for sale. This will enable you to develop a business profile that will attract buyers – and maintain their interest until completion, and build into the business those aspects that will encourage a buyer to increase their bid. This book will take you through the sale process: preparation, marketing, acceptance of offer, the due diligence examination (the vendor's nightmare), successful completion, and beyond.

ISBN 978-1-84528-328-5

HOW TO RUN A GREAT HOTEL

ENDA M LARKIN

This book is based on the premise that being good is just not good enough in today's competitive environment. For hotel owners and managers who want to achieve lasting business success through a root and branch review of key business processes, this easy to read, practical, and action oriented *book is a 'must read'*. It will serve as a personal business consultant for the hotel professional, probing and testing their thinking across five critical themes which are proven to drive excellence. The content focuses less on day-to-day operations and more on big picture concerns such as strategy development, enhancing leadership skills, engaging employees and attaining customer focus, all of which are central to building a great hotel.

ISBN 978-1-84528-346-9

HOW TO START AND RUN A FISH AND CHIP SHOP OR BURGER BAR

JAMES KAYUI LI

This book offers detailed guidance on how to spot a good location for your premises and how to fit it out. Everything you need to know is here: the advantages and disadvantages of freehold versus a leasehold business; the practice and importance of food hygiene; employing staff, advertising, VAT and book-keeping and even recommended frying and cooking methods.

ISBN 978-1-84528-308-7

How To Books are available through all good bookshops, or you can order direct from us through Grantham Book Services.

Tel: +44 (0)1476 541080
Fax: +44 (0)1476 541061
Email: orders@gbs.tbs-ltd.co.uk

Or via our website

www.howtobooks.co.uk

To order via any of these methods please quote the title(s) of the book(s) and your credit card number together with its expiry date.

For further information about our books and catalogue, please contact:

How To Books
Spring Hill House
Spring Hill Road
Begbroke
Oxford
OX5 1RX

Visit our web site at

www.howtobooks.co.uk

Or you can contact us by email at info@howtobooks.co.uk